# TREVOR DENTON'S
Classic Football Terrace Reading

# TO THE TERRACES BORN

A STORY OF SOCCER VIOLENCE FROM THE MID-60'S TO THE PRESENT TIME. THE PASSION, LOVE, LIVES, AND CAMARADERIE OF KINDRED SPIRITS EVERYWHERE!

Pen Press Publishers Ltd

First published in Great Britain by
Pen Press Publishers Ltd
39-41, North Road
Islington
London N7 9DP


ISBN 1-904018-46-7


Printed and bound in the UK


A catalogue record of this book is available from the British
Library


Cover design Jacqueline Abromeit
Photo Coloursport

# Contents

Introduction and Acknowledgements

## Introduction and Acknowledgements

Trevor Denton (aliasT.D.) would like to thank Max and Garb and their tribe for the endless cups of coffee and tea and cans of Stella and Fosters, and for their encouragement and support of this project. Particular thanks must go to the General for helping me to remember what happened, and the research into the true events that have been written about in this book. Also great thanks must go to Bob for getting this work-of-art published, forever blue!

TREV

## Dedication

This book is dedicated with all my love always to Jackie,
Charlotte and Rhiannon.
I am also very grateful to those friends and persons, whom
without, this book would never have been written. God
bless you all, you know who you are!


## Tribute

On 11 February 2003, Micky Dunn (alias Sticky) lost his
brave battle with cancer. A true Chelsea fan to the end - his
coffin entered the packed church to the glorious tune of
'Chelsea, Chelsea'.

He will be missed.

## Names and  Faces

1.    Graham Gamage - alias Garb or The General.
2.    Ian Cox - (not to be confused with Ian Cox, number 7).
3.    Guy - Coxy's brother.
4.    Pete Jefferys - Butcher.
5.    (The infamous) Micky Dunn - alias Sticky Bunn - ticket tout extraordinaire.
6.    (The one and only) Paul Reeves - alias Match. Also brothers Andy and Mark.
7.    Ian Cox - alias Bimbo. (National Hunt jockey supreme - he of Freight Forwarder and Snowtown-Boy fame! Tips straight from the horse's mouth.
8.    Angus and his lovely wife Anna. (God bless his cotton socks - and hers!)
9.    Andy Warren. (Where would we be without Andy!)
10.   Roger Mapp - alias Mappe.
11.   Steve Hickmott - alias Hickey (No. 1).
12.   Dave Wolvey and Marcus.
13.   Clifford Bolton.
14.   Graham Haines - alias Ferret.
15.   Mick and Debbie (The Kelsey Arms).
16.   Paul and Gary Collins.
17.   Bisal (rum and blackcurrant please).
18.   Charlie (Tunbridge Wells).
19.   Jock.
20.   Spud Taylor.

21. Richard and Christine. (The longbow, Tunbridge Wells). Also Darren, Stockholm, Sweden, Cup winners Final 1-5-98.
22. Mo Johnson - alias Mogy (alias Kim Johnson).
23. Chub.
24. Scranner. (Likes Man. Utd but loves Chelsea?!) Why?
25. Bob Harbour (has anyone got a spare ticket? If not, I'll get in anyway!)
26. Vernon.
27. Hitler (who I met in Spain after a decade - 1970's Chelsea).
28. Paul Baitup.
29. Tom The Hod (wherever you may be!)
30. Danny Harkans - alias Eccles (great times, great memories - thanks for the teaching school).
31. Colin Daniels (landlord extraordinaire).
32. Babs - the one and only.
33. Sean - nice pub, nice card school.
34. Sean O'Callaghan.
35. The crew of (The Roebuck), Tunbridge Wells, where many a mission was planned and many journeys began from.
36. Mr Connie Butler Esq.
37. Paul Gabril.
38. Besa. (Tonbridge) and Jeff Moss.
39. Alex.
40. Alex (Chick) - Sherry-Sue.
41. Italian Danny - of Danny's Cafe fame. Likes Chelsea but prefers Juventus and Inter-Milan, (understandable!)
42. Simon (lost at a young age but a good mate).
43. Mr Lingfield (re. Bobby Harbour) Les.
44. Steve (Southborough) Bridges (re. Ferret).
45. Jonesey, Chelsea 1970's, Switzerland!
46. Dartford Trevor and son.
47. Harpo (re. Bobby Harbour) Roebuck.
48. Brixton Charlie and Finney.

49. Mark Whitehead.
50. Tracy Woods.
51. Bonehead.
52. Mick Greenaway.
53. Mad Kev (Kevin) Tunbridge Wells.
54. Bob Desautels (Chelsea 'till I die!)
55. John Francis (JF).
56. Kim Styles (disc-jockey extraordinaire).
57. The Liquidator (mainstream).
58. Garrison (thanks for keeping the faith).
59. Agnetha and Inger (Sweden) a big thank you.
60. Bob Lawrence. Trout fisherman and publisher extraordinaire.

And anyone else that contributed to this masterpiece in anyway, cheers TD.

Joshua was a great leader of the Israelites
Joshua's army conquered the city of Jericho
they marched around the city
they shouted and blew trumpets,
and God made the walls of Jericho fall down

JOSHUA v.5-6

# CHAPTER 1

## EARLY DOORS, THE START

I have asked myself this question, not once, but perhaps a hundred times and I keep coming to the same conclusion. After a lot of soul-searching, this anger, violence, passion and love inside of me comes from deep-bent emotions and from my roots of existence.

Although my father liked football and was also a follower of Chelsea Football Club, I never went to "The Bridge" with him, it was just coincidence that we followed the same team.

I now know where and why my support of Chelsea comes from, which is to be explained later in this book.

Imagine, if you can, being brought up in the mid 60's on a council estate, somewhere in Middle Class England. Loving family - great mother and father, both working hard to support the family and trying hard to make ends meet. Neil Armstrong was still to walk on the moon, a pint of bitter cost 11p (2/2d), a packet of fags 29p (5/10d), a newspaper 2p (5d) and the price of a three-bed semi-detached house was about £5,500. The family car, an Escort or a Mini, would cost about £700 and the music you would be listening to would probably have been The Rolling Stones, The Beatles, or The Who - if you were a bloke that is!

Oh yes, we must not forget, England were just about to have their finest moment on the green and hallowed turf of Wembley. Ah! Blissful days indeed! Will we ever see the likes of that again? I doubt it, but we can all live in hope! Anyhow, back to the plot...

I knew of Graham (Garb - the General) from my secondary school days, when we all used to kick a tennis ball around in the playground and go around in gangs. I am a couple of years older. It was not until we had left school that we really became close friends and this happened merely by chance.

We have stayed mates ever since, despite marriages, divorces and children coming along for both of us. We still live within a mile of each other, in the same town, and I am sure that if we cut ourselves it would be blue blood that would be shed and not red. The General's mother, Pam, was a ladies hairdresser on the estate where we lived. My mother used to go to her house to get her hair done, as it meant she didn't have to make a long journey into town. One day, whilst having her hair done, Garb's mum happened to mention that her son liked football. It was from that moment that a long friendship with Garb was secured.

Saturday afternoons were never to be the same again, we would sit by the television set watching David Coleman introduce Grandstand on BBC1, and Kenneth Wolstenholme introducing the football review, long before Sky, Digital and cable TV were ever thought of. Garb and I were hooked on Kenneth's every word, and we looked forward to watching him every Saturday lunchtime. Afterwards, we would go to the local park on our estate to play football, often pretending to be the players talked about in that lunchtime programme. Magic moments indeed! We were also joined in the park by the likes of Bob Harbour, Pete Jefferys and Match. This is where their friendship comes from, I am sure of that. Next, what team to follow? Liverpool, Arsenal or Manchester United? The choice was ours. Most of these teams seemed to be winning week in, week out, and one of them was always top, or near the top of the First Division. Yes, I did say First Division, no Premiership in those early years. It had to be Liverpool, surely, as they were playing in Europe as well as the First Division-Europe! Where was that? In those far off days, Europe seemed as far away as the moon. How times change! But no, not Liverpool, Arsenal or Manchester United for the General and myself, it had to be Chelsea as our team to follow and support. Why? Simple really, Chelsea always seemed to be the great under-achievers, losing by the odd goals here and there, it brought out the Great British underdog spirit in us. Not only that, but when we watched the Saturday evening match reports on Grandstand, it always seemed that something happened in the match involving Chelsea that went against them. Not a lot has changed there, then! So, Chelsea it was.

Stamford Bridge, their ground, was the place to go, however, it was to be a couple of years before myself the General, Pete Jefferys, Match and Bobby Harbour were to go to the Mecca follow the Holy Grail and experience "Terrace Life" in the First Division, first hand. South West London was a few years away yet!

After yet another game of football in our local park, the General suggested that we go and watch our local team on a Saturday afternoon, the idea seemed a good one, so off we went and "Terrace Life" was born. Two buses and 6d later we were there at Culverden Stadium, the home of our local team the Tunbridge Wells Rangers of

2

the Southern League. Attendance was anything from the mind-boggling crowd of 30 people (plus dogs), including turnstile attendants and half-time serving staff, to a maximum of 200-plus, depending on who the Rangers were playing at the time. The mighty Merthyr Tydfil, Barry Town, Stevenage Borough, the list of all the greats is endless!

The first match we watched was Tunbridge Wells Rangers against Merthyr-Tydfil, from Wales (yes, Wales). Merthyr had brought at least 10 supporters with them on their long treck, and were they about to get some stick and abuse from the local fans! In those days the Southern League meant southern, no divisional sections, hours of travel for the teams.

Yeovil in Somerset, Barry Town and Merthyr-Tydfil in Wales, Hinckley in the East-Midlands, these were the sort of distances clubs had to travel. Often turning up with only half an hour to spare, and then having to play a full match before travelling back the same afternoon or evening.

As it happened, Merthyr had arrived at about 2.30 in the afternoon, got changed and out on to the pitch by 2.50 ready for the 3 o'clock kick-off. Both myself and Garb were in place behind the home goal after paying our turnstile fee of 15p (3d), plus about 2p for a programme. This was where the home supporters seemed to congregate - all 30 of them plus a few dogs! Merthyr were out on the pitch having a kick about, when suddenly the loud speakers, which for the past hour had been playing marching band music, blared out the Rolling Stones number "Honky Tonk Women", to which the majestic Tunbridge Wells Rangers strolled out onto the pitch. There was rapturous applause, followed by much laughter as one of the players tripped over a rut in the pitch. On closer inspection, it appeared that the pitch had ruts and holes all over it, Wembley it wasn't!!! In fact, I think a local farmer grazed his animals on it during the week. Anyhow, the match started and by half-time Tunbridge Wells were 3-0 down. The bloke standing next to me had been shouting abuse at the opposition for the first 45 minutes, chants such as "Go back to your coal mines you Welsh bastards" and "I bet you shag sheep". Garb and I thought this highly amusing. We later found out that he was a permanent fixture at the Culverden stadium, and was considered to be the local nutter, his name was Bonehead.

The second half began, and the Rangers started attacking strongly, looking for a goal to get back into the match, unfortunately, to no avail. Bonehead was getting louder and louder and his voice could be heard all over the ground - and also on the pitch! The Merthyr centre half, whose name eludes me at the moment, but I think it was Jones (well, they're all Jones from Wales - aren't they?!) had already been booked once for a flying tackle on the Wells centre-forward. He then nearly cut the centre-forward in half with another vicious tackle that had no place on a football pitch. By this time Bonehead was having a baby, going completely mental, - "Send the Welsh cunt off, Ref" and "I'm going to punch your fucking head in, you Welsh shithead." Very patriotic was Bonehead, as I remember him!

The Referee went over to the offending Welsh player and sent him off, much to the great amusement of Bonehead and the rest of us. Rangers lost 4-0, but that didn't seem to matter to me at the time, Garb and I had a good time chanting with Bonehead, - even though we didn't know what all the swearwords meant!

After the match Jones (the Merthyr player sent off) made a beeline towards Bonehead in the crowd, which wasn't too hard, as most of the people had made their way home before the end of the match. Garb and I thought that this 6'6" Welshman made mountain was going to find Bonehead and kick him, but no! He found Bonehead and asked him, "Was it you, son, giving me stick all through the game? Bonehead (not wishing to lose face with the locals) replied in a squeaky voice, "Yeah, what are you going to do about it?" Garb and I thought, this is it, Bonehead's just about to have his brains knocked out. But, to our amazement, Jones said, "Put it there, son," and held out his hand in a gesture of friendship. Bonehead nervously shook his hand, thankful for not losing his reputation in front of his mates. Jones then told him, "I love getting stick - it makes me play so much better! I hope when we play you next time that you are here - be lucky!"

On the bus home that evening, Garb and I thought what a great afternoon out it had been and we couldn't wait for the next match at the Culverden, and to meet up with Bonehead again. Yes, on those old railway sleepers behind the home goal in the early 60's, that Tunbridge Wells called terraces, it happened. Terrace Life was definitely born in Garb and me, and I will be forever grateful to Bonehead, whatever happened to him? I wonder.

# CHAPTER 2

## CHELSEA, THE ROEBUCK YEARS

After a few years of going to the Culverden and following Rangers, Garb and I were getting a bit fed up and bored with listening to Bonehead ranting and raving every Saturday. In fact, the usual crowd were looking to Garb and myself for a bit of fun and a laugh. It appeared that we had taken over from Bonehead as the main attractions! But Garb and I wanted more. - We had to have a sit down and rethink our future plans. The Mecca it was! Chelsea here we come!!!

We needed a base to work from - The Roebuck it was! The Roebuck was a public house in the centre of our town, Tunbridge Wells in Kent. Garb and I were just starting to discover drinking, drugs and girls as pleasures and pastimes (but not necessarily in that order). In those days pubs shut at 10.30 pm, but The Roebuck allowed "after hours" drinking, and a lot of the youngsters in the town went there, so that was the pub for us. The jukebox in the pub had a lot of good sounds on it, but two stand out in my mind. The first was Sam and Dave's "Soul man" which developed into a great soul classic. Many a relationship started listening to this tune, - notably between myself and a girl called Alex and between Garb and two birds Sherry and Sue. These girls had flats in the town and many a time we would go back to their places to crash out after too much beer or drugs. No questions were asked, so these women were ideal people to look after us and bring us back down to earth after a heavy session!

The other memorable tune was "Liquidator" by Harry J and The All Stars, it had a great chorus line, which could be repeated as "Chelsea, Chelsea" and was adopted by the Chelsea Shed, but it originated from The Roebuck and that's a fact, according to our local DJ Kim Styles!

Another tune adopted was Zigger, zagger, zigger, zagger, oi, oi,oi, - a Micky Greenaway chant, a Shedman's song, soon to find its way to all football grounds. In the sixties "Liquidator" was mine and Garb's song. It was a great sight to see the Chelsea Shed and the rest of Stamford Bridge swaying and singing to the tune. When I hear the song now, it still makes me tremble with excitement. I can still see The

Shed crowd in my mind. It was a magical sight to behold if you were True Blue!!

Tunbridge Wells, where the General and myself lived, was a Chelsea stronghold in the south of England, as well as Tonbridge, Leatherhead, Epsom and Dorking. There were quite a few other towns, too numerous to mention, - but all full of nutters!

Back to The Roebuck, it was soon developing into a Chelsea fans pub. I don't exactly know why, perhaps it was because of its reputation as a good-time pub. The place to be seen, it certainly was for the General and me.

Other people who frequented The Roebuck in those early years were Micky Dunn (sticky bun), who was the local ticket tout and still is! Any ticket for any match, Micky could get you at a price! Sitting in the corner of the pub was usually Bisal, rum and blackcurrant in his hand or dribbling down his chin. Bisal was much like Micky, selling tickets, flags and T-shirts and they often used to work together. Then, of course, there was Hickey, what a great man, Steve Hickmott. The national press had a field day with Hickey, first The Daily Mirror, then The Sun, then they all jumped in. Hickey even appeared on the television as "the most feared football hooligan in England", a more vicious and violent thug you could not wish to meet. But we loved him and still do. Hickey was the original No. 1 "Chelsea Head-hunter", and we all followed him whatever he did, Packy bashing, police baiting, we were all behind him. If there was a fight to be had we were there.

On many occasions Hickey led an army of 500 people, marching through towns which were populated with Packis or blacks, giving Nazi salutes and singing racial threats. We would then break ranks and smash down Paki shopkeepers, doors, and hurl bricks through their windows and then loot the shops. No one could take on the Chelsea Head-hunters! We were considered No.1 on the thug list. Other clubs tried to take us on, but to no avail. The Chelsea Head-hunters ran from no one.

Oh how I love Hickey for what he taught us all. We used to get a few bloody faces and a few good kickings, but that was all part of the fun.

Hickey was nicked eventually. An early morning raid by the police from Scotland Yard led to him doing some time. He got out early and later had the police for wrongful imprisonment. Yeah! Hickey had a big trial at the Old Bailey. I think that the police wanted to make an example of a football thug and Hickey, and the likes of Ginger Terry, fitted the bill nicely, thank you! It was the Prime Minister, Maggie (May), Thatcher's way of showing she had her finger on the pulse, where football violence was concerned.

Hickey got a 10 year sentence, but after two and a half years he and the others were released and their convictions were torn to pieces. Fucking Old Bill, fiddling the facts and tampering with evidence. Typical! Hickey and the lads got loads of dosh out of it all, and I think that the damages awarded were something like £150,000 to £200,000 a piece. Nice work if you can get it. The officers who fitted Hickey up got away with a bollocking from their superiors, typical Old Bill protecting their own and closing ranks when needed. This whole affair was what the press, media and police nicknamed "Operation Own Goal"!!! Hickey now owns a bar in Bangkok called "The Dog's Bollocks", and we still keep in contact via the internet. The last time I met him, he was kicking a few Cockney Reds (Manchester United fans) from London, who had never been to Old Trafford in their life. Things don't change, and I hope for God's sake Hickey never does.

Hickey's No.2 was Dave Wolvey, another Roebuck man, and Hickey's tactical planner. He would plan where we were going to hit and where we would encounter the opposition. Perhaps this was the way Churchill planned England's movements in the war! But we found Dave's methods worked for us Head-hunters - always looking for and finding trouble and aggro. Then there was Angus, what can I say about Angus and his lovely wife Anna? Only that Angus lived about 200 yards from The Roebuck and could drink 15 to 20 pints of lager and half a bottle of Scotch within 3-4 hours and still talk sensibly. How he isn't dead by now, I don't know. He must have no blood left inside him, just lager and whisky! However, he was just the person you wanted beside you when the fighting started. Whenever we hit a town for a match, the first person you would see was Angus with a half empty bottle of Scotch in his hand, wandering about. Whether it was 6 in the morning or midday, you could always be sure of meeting him. How he got to places like Wigan, Hereford, Carlisle or Exeter, I don't know, because he very rarely travelled with the rest of the crew. He would always greet us with the line, "I've found a great little pub for us lads, which was always good to hear because the first place we wanted, after a long train journey, was a pub we could call ours. The landlords would usually let us have the run of their pub as they didn't want their establishment smashed to pieces. It all started quietly, but as the match approached we were often serving ourselves from behind the bar and giving out free booze, fags and food to our mates. One such occasion was down in Hereford where we all invaded this particular little country pub. The landlord wondered what was happening in his nice little pub being surrounded by 30 mad Chelsea supporters, but he was quite happy for us to spend our money. As time went on, more and more Chelsea supporters were coming into the pub. Everyone was drinking the local scrumpy (cider) and getting very, very drunk. It was really strong stuff. The landlord reckoned that nobody could drink more than a couple of pints, and how right he was! The cider was so thick you could almost see the apples drifting about in the glass, the locals wouldn't drink it, but that didn't stop us loonies. After a few hours of drinking the usual thing happened in the pub and we were all serving ourselves, but the landlord didn't seem to mind as his pub was not getting smashed up. About an hour before kick off everyone decided to make their way to the ground. However, Match, the General and I never made it to the ground or the game, but spent the afternoon collapsed and being very ill in the local graveyard, as I recall. I think Chelsea lost 4-0, but that didn't matter. One thing's for sure, I won't drink scrumpy from that neck of the woods again. No wonder the locals never drank the stuff, it was lethal. The local plod in these towns never used to worry us too much, as they knew that all the time we were pissed we wouldn't start to make trouble. They kept a low profile - even when provoked. There were times when police horses were hit in the head by snooker balls nicked from the pubs, this was a favourite trick. It was rare that the police would retaliate but when they did it was a fun time seeing how many plod you could knock down and kick.

This was all part of the day out. You lived on the memories and told your mates about it until the next time it happened.

Angus's wife, the lovely Anna, was much like Angus in many respects. She too could hold her liquor (and still can). She is the salt of the earth and was a mother figure to all The Roebuck lads, often providing a shoulder to cry on, or a bed for the night (not literally) and a good hot meal. A great lady, Anna, thank you very much! Other fringe players from The Roebuck days were Clifford Bolton, Les Lingfield, Chub and Marcus. I never knew Chub's real name but everyone called him Chub, so his nickname stuck. I was once in the Kop End at Anfield, back in the early sixties, and Chelsea were getting stuffed 4-0. There were a lot of little skirmishes going on all through the match between Kopites and Chelsea Head-hunters, when, all of a sudden, there was a parting of the waves, like Moses in the Bible when he parted the Red Sea. I looked up and about 2,000 people in the Kop had parted and there I could see Bobby Harbour, Clifford and Marcus standing at the top of the Kop terrace with blood stream-ing down their faces. They were shouting at the top of their voices, "Come on you fucking northern bastards, let's have you," and with that they charged from the top to the bottom, kicking and lashing out as they went. The Liverpool supporters just parted and let them through, right into the arms of the police, who were waiting for them at the bottom. Bob, Clifford and Marcus were thrown out of the ground, but they managed to get back in again before the end of the match, which in those days was very easy to do. If you got thrown out of the ground by the local plod, you could wait a little while and then jump over the nearest turnstiles. The Old Bill never used to arrest anyone back in the 60's, they must have thought that we were all nut-ters and mad southerners, which we were, especially Bobby, Clifford and Marcus. I've never seen anything like that on the terraces before, where a home team did not just run, but completely split into two sections. It was certainly a magic moment in terrace violence. I heard Liverpool supporters saying, "Don't go near them, they've got guns and knives," but Bob, Clifford and Marcus just had their fists and Doc Martens! The Scousers (Liverpool) just shit their pants!!

Chelsea's proud reputation as the hardest thugs in the league and country was growing. The only time I can remember getting a good hiding was against (of all teams) Tottenham. This happened back in the 1974-75 season, when Chelsea were in the second division. The match was at White Hart Lane, where Spurs play, and Chelsea were all in the Park Lane end. This was also where most of the Spurs sup-porters were as well as in the Shelf end. The fighting and battles went from the terraces and spilt out on to the pitch. But then, what hap-pened, I don't know, because Chelsea got murdered that day.

The match was refereed by Jack Walker, who was a butcher from the Midlands. I remember him walking out to the centre of the pitch while both sets of warring fans were fighting and kicking the hell out of each other. But Chelsea certainly got a good kicking that day, and when the history of the terrace is written, that game will be Chelsea's blackest day. When Chelsea got promotion to the top flight again, the Government tried to stop Chelsea fans by banning them from going to away games. The Minister for Sport at that time was MP Dennis

Howell, a right prat!!! He wouldn't have known a football fan if he was sitting on one. Everyone at Stamford Bridge had T-shirts with the words, "You can't ban a Chelsea fan", printed on them, they were the things to wear! Micky Dunn and Bisal were making a killing flogging them. So the Government were going to ban us from away grounds. Oh Yeah!! Their great idea was to only sell tickets to season ticket holders, shareholders and members of official supporters clubs, oh yes, and to loyal supporters whose behaviour could be guaranteed. Well thought out by the Ministry, so what did we all do? Easy, we all just became members, that really stopped us from going to away matches, didn't it??! I think not!!

The General and myself could have come up with a better plan, I think even Bobby Harbour and Angus could have too!!! (Even when Angus was pissed). How do these top dogs get these jobs? I wish I knew, it's got to be more than 'the old school tie' thing, it amazes me!!

So it was now decided to put a ban on all us Chelsea fans from going to away games, after all the recent fighting and bloodshed and aggro at other grounds, and good old Maggie (May) Thatcher, the then Prime Minister, and the MP for sport, Dennis-Howell, came up with this plan of attack. OH YEAH! What a great idea, that was really going to stop us following our beloved Chelsea wasn't it, I THINK NOT!!!

I think who ever came up with that brainwave, must have had the intelligence of a chocolate frog, to say the least! And they rule our country, GOD HELP THE REST OF US, that's all I can say!

The general idea was to only sell tickets for games to loyal fans (JOKE!) season-ticket holders and members of the supporters club. Consequently, at the next home match at the Bridge there was a huge queue to the box-office, which stretched nearly to Fulham-Broadway tube station. People were queuing to get application forms for membership. The people behind the jump (counter) in the box-office could not believe their luck, suddenly there were hundreds and hundreds of loons and crazies wanting to become members.

I recall good old Pete-Jeffreys, who by this time was plying his trade as a Butcher in Tunbridge Wells, and Andy-Warren, who was plying his trade as a drunk in Tunbridge Wells, waiting in the queue for hours to get hold of these forms. In the evening they came into The Roebuck, and handed the application forms to us to fill in. The forms were all duly filled in and signed, even Clifford-Bolton a complete crazy and nutter, but a great bloke and Chelsea through and through, managed to become a club member. Incredibly, as a more hardened thug than Clifford, you would wish not to meet, Clifford is now a pillar of society, and teaches underprivileged kids. Still, it just goes to prove a leopard occasionally can change his spots. When I was last speaking to Clifford he was telling me about how he still yearns for the thrill of the ruck and the fighting on the terraces and surrounding streets. I suppose you can take the boy out of the man, but you cannot take the man out of the boy! Or if you like, you can take Chelsea from the boy, but you cannot take Chelsea from the MAN! Yes, Clifford has certainly turned full circle in more senses than one. Have a spliff for me Cliff!!

A wait of between three weeks to a month, then we received little blue identity cards with our names and photos on them. We were now all official supporters club members. YIPPEE!! Complete bullshit. All it meant to us Tunbridge Wells was that we could legally get hold of match tickets for away games. We had done what we had set out to do. In fact, it was now much easier to get tickets. A big thank you must got to Maggie Thatcher and Dennis Howell for such a gigantic cock-up. While I was researching this book, I came across my old membership card, along with an old T-shirt with, "YOU CAN'T BAN A CHELSEA FAN" printed on it. I remember to this day Micky-Dunn and Bisal walking into The Roebuck one Saturday night, throwing four large black bin liners on the floor, and Micky shouting to everyone in the pub, "YOUR SIZE IS IN THERE SOME-WHERE. They're two quid each." Micky and Bisal had had hundreds of T-shirts printed and were flogging them like hot cakes, never ones to miss out on making a quick buck were Mr Michael-Dunn and his partner in crime Bisal. We were all wearing our newly acquired T-shirts around Tunbridge Wells, for a few weeks and months. I'm sure the good folk of the Wells did not know what to make of it all! I was quite often asked what the words on the front meant, and I tried to explain to people, in my own way. I don't think people understood where I was coming from, but who fucking cared anyway. Not me, that's for sure, or any other Roebuck crew members. Micky and Bisal continued selling the T-shirts all over the place especially outside Stamford-Bridge on Match days. Soon nearly everyone in the Shed and North-Stand had one on. It was seen at the time as a statement against the Government, but just like in later years, T-shirts with "WHO THE F—K ARE MAN UTD" printed on them, became a fashion item down the Fulham Road. I am sure this is where Sticky and Bisal started their business supplying black market tickets. It is all that I have ever known Micky and Bisal to do in the thirty-plus years that I have known them. A right couple of entrepreneurs!! I have only ever known them selling tickets, sweatshirts, T-shirts and travel arrangements. Oh yes, and of course, the odd trip or two to bring back cigarettes and alcohol, and the excursions to our friends in Holland for the wackey-baccy and other stuff! No my memory must be playing me up again, Micky "DID" have a real job! Back in the early seventies as I recall, working for good old British Rail. He worked in a track-gang laying and repairing the rails, but two weeks collar (work) was enough for Micky. He hasn't got his hands dirty since! Not bad for a bloke coming up shortly to his fiftieth year. Like they say, they threw away the mould when they made that one. In Micky's case, those few spoken words certainly are true, a truly great bloke and a close friend Mr Michael-Dunn Esq. Bisal, on the other hand, is Mickey's eyes and mouth. Whereas Micky, on the odd occasion, might let a deal or opportunity slip by him, Bisal would turn every last chance in to earning a pound, to his advantage. He still does to this day, hence why Bisal drives around in a flash Mercedes and lives in a big house in the leafy stockbroker belt of Surrey. Mick's still using Shanks's pony (walking). The early bonding of friendship, will always be there between the two self-made entrepreneurs. Perhaps, instead of being known as Micky and Bisal, we could start to call the pair of them, Del and Rodney. Perhaps this season Micky will get his arse back down to the local T-shirt shop and get some T-shirts printed, with the words "CHELSEA F.C. Premier League CHAMPIONS 200?". Oh well, perhaps not then, yes, as my darling wife has just reminded me, "I WAS ONLY DREAMING," and that was a pink pig that just flew past my window, wasn't it! Ban a Chelsea fan, the British Government have more chance of meeting little green men from the planet "ZOG", enough said. It was chucking out time in The Roebuck, well, one thirty in the morning anyhow, when dear old Angus turned to me and said, "Come on TREV, are you coming?"

To which I replied, "I'll see you in the club in a minute," thinking he was on the march to our local nightclub in Tunbridge Wells at the time. How 'WRONG' could I be, he was only setting off for Chelsea's next encounter. It was only Wednesday evening or was it Thursday morning, I wasn't quite sure, as I was quite pissed at the time of Angus's question. Anyhow it was a couple of days before Saturday, I knew that. Work would have to be put on hold for a few days. In fact, fuck the work! It never really seemed to matter in those halcyon days.

Chelsea Football Club was much more important to me than any job. Come to think about it, they still are, but priorities change a little bit the older you get e.g. marriage, the wife, kids, houses, etc.

"Right Angus, I'm right with you," I said to him, "where are we going?"

"BLACKPOOL," came the reply, to which my reply to Angus was something like, "Fuck me ANGUS, you're having a bloody laugh, it's nearly two o'clock in the morning. "Coming or not, Trev?"

"Yeah, let's go then!"

Angus had his work's van (a rusty old Ford transit), with over 150 thousand miles on the clock, parked up in the pub's forecourt. This was going to be our transport to the golden sand and seaside town of Blackpool. I turned to Angus and said "Hold on a minute mate, you can't drive and neither can I. We have both had too much (shant) beer. We need more recruits and reinforcements and a driver." I looked around the pub, and shouted to everyone who was still in the bars, "ME AND ANGUS ARE OFF TO BLACKPOOL, ANY OF YOU TOSSERS UP FOR IT?" Suddenly, we had about another dozen or so people joining us for the away day trip. Two of the people who said they would come with us, volunteered to take it in turns with the driving. They were Harpo, so nicknamed by all us lads because of his hair and facial features which reminded us of the famous Marx brother, and Chub, so called because his facial features resembled a fish! No not really!! In fact, I never knew why we did call him Chub. In fact,I never knew his real name in twenty-five odd years. The pair of them where true-blues, and that was always good enough for me. Besides, they where the only ones sober in the pub. Harpo had his own building company specialising in plastering and still does to this day. Chub is in the music business as a public-relations man, for a small record company in London. Some old mattresses and blankets where quickly gathered together and thrown into the back of Angus's trannie, just for kipping down and, of course, also in the hope that we might pick up a couple of old slappers between Tunbridge Wells and Blackpool (you never knew your luck). So off we set, on yet another adventure in the life of a Chelsea supporter. We had only gone about a mile from the pub, when I shouted to Harpo, who was driving at the time, to stop at the next telephone box. Don't forget this was years before mobile phones where thought of! The trannie came to a halt I jumped out of the back doors. I shouted to the rest of the lads, "I won't be a minute. I've got an important call to make," This to cries of "Hurry up Trev, "We're fucking freezing in here," and "who the fuck are you ringing up at three in the morning?"

"You'll find out soon tossers," came my reply, and I jumped back into the transit. I then directed Harpo around a few streets in Tunbridge Wells and five minutes later, we had arrived at where I wanted to be. "Toot the van's horn a few times, Harpo," I said, and he did.

Bedroom lights came on at the house we stopped outside, and the bedroom window opened, "Give me two minutes and I will be with you," came the reply!

"Who are we picking up now? Trev asked Harpo.

"You'll see," I said. With that the van doors opened up again, and in jumped the General (Garb) I mean, how could we go all the way to sunny Blackpool without the General!! No chance!!

"Fuck me, Trev. I jumped out of my skin when the phone went off, I was just giving Sherry a good seeing too!"

"Never mind, mate. There will be plenty of time for shagging when we get back home," I said to him. "And just think about all those northern slags that'll be up for it."

"Yeah, Trev, foot down hard Harpo, Blackpool here we come," shouted Garb. With the General on board, we finally left Tunbridge Wells behind us and we started the long trek north. Time for a little sleep in the back of the van, and let Harpo continue the driving, I told myself. Sherry, the General's girlfriend at that time, was, as I recall, quite understanding about Garb leaving her in the middle of the night, so he could come to football, or so I thought!

A few weeks later, we were all drinking and standing around in The Roebuck and reminiscing about the previous week's battles and looking forward to new encounters when the door of the pub burst open and in walked Sherry. She made a beeline straight for the General and shouted at him these chosen words, "YOU THINK MORE OF THIS PUB THAN YOU DO OF ME, YOU BASTARD." Then she threw a plate of hot roast dinner all over him, gravy and all, which she had brought into the pub with her. How we all laughed at the General's misfortune, as I'm sure you can imagine? Funny, but nobody clapped eyes on Sherry after that little incident. Oh well, ships that pass in the night and all that. In those days, if a bird gave you grief you would soon 'out her' (get rid of her). There was always an abundance to be found hanging around the pubs and clubs we all used to haunt! So picking up the next conquest was never too much of a problem! Shame about Sherry though nice girl and very largr tits as I recall and excellent in the sack, according to Garb. Still, like I say, football and Chelsea come first, that's just the way it is, and always will be, for myself and the General, thank God!!

Harpo continued driving through the night, taking it in turns at the wheel with Chub. By now, I had managed to sober up a little bit, so I took my turn also at the wheel. It was now beginning to get very sweaty and smelly in the trannie, everybody farting and dropping their guts from the previous night's drinking and the drinking that was still going on! A couple of cases of beer had been thrown into the back of the van when the blankets and mattresses were loaded on. The windows to the trannie were fully opened now and dawn was just breaking. Angus's old eight-track stereo was blasting out songs by Slade, (good old Noddy) and T-Rex and, of course, Rodney. Everyone was by now waking up and in full voice, and, as per usual, was also wondering where the fuck they were!! And the old nutmeg of, "When are we going to stop for food?" (Breakfast). I was still driving, and all I kept hearing in my ear was, "Trev," pull up over at the next greasy-spoon you see, we're all fucking starving in the back here." By now we were heading up the M1, so I decided to pull off the motorway and find a transport cafe somewhere on a B road. After a couple of miles the General spotted a sign "JOE'S DINER" that was good enough for me and the rest of the lads. We pulled into a large gravel car park which was half full of juggernauts and truckers. I then shouted to everyone, "ALL OUT, GRUB'S UP." All the heroes stumbled out of the trannie and into the cafe to get the bacon, eggs beans and a fried slice, etc down their throats. After we had washed all the grub down with cups of tea and coffee, it was time to go on our merry way again, or so I thought! 'WRONG', I threw the van keys to another member of our entourage, Mr Paul Collins who had volunteered to do a bit of the driving. Paul put the keys into the van's ignition, turned the engine and nothing happened, tried again and again and still nothing! We were stuck in Joe's diner car park. We all had our heads under the bonnet of Angus's transit as if we knew what we were looking for, but really no one had a clue, not even Angus himself knew what was wrong with his old rust-bucket. "FUCKING BRILLIANT," I thought to myself! "What do we do now," I asked the General who was standing beside me at the time.

Then, someone had the brainwave to go back into Joe's Diner and ask the truckers. "GREAT IDEA," I said, "give that man a biscuit!" So me and the General marched back into the cafe and started to ask about. After about twenty minutes, we got a result, a couple of truckers from 'Jockland', (Scotland) said they would have a look at the sick trannie after they had devoured their breakfast. Me and the General went back outside to tell the rest of the party that we had got a result. True to their word, after about half an hour, the two Jocks appeared. They both walked slowly over the cafe car park, where our dead transit stood. "WHAT'S WRONG WITH HER, THEN, LADIES," said one of the Jocks. I was having a piss behind a nearby tree, when Angus, who was also having a piss, shouted out, "IF WE KNEW WHAT WAS WRONG, WE WOULDN'T BE ASKING YOU, YOU SCOTTISH WANKERS."

I very quickly told Angus to shut his mouth up, as these two Jocks were all the hope we had between Joe's Diner car park and BLACK-POOL. For once in his life, I think he understood where I was coming from and took my advice! Luckily for us, the two Jocks never heard him. We must have been just out of ear-shot range. That piss certainly saved our bacon to coin a phase. "I think it might be an electrical fault," said the General to one of the Jocks.

"Aye laddie, is that so," replied one of our new found Scottish friends. "Well, lift up the wee bonnet and let a couple of old truckers have a look then, if you would be so kind," they said. With that, the trannie's bonnet was opened yet again, and the two Jocks both peered inside at the engine. The General, by the way, was about this time halfway through a five year apprenticeship to become an electrician, which after about thirty years, he is just getting to grips with. I'm only joking! In fact, Garb, the General, is a shit-hot sparky (electrician). With all his different exam papers and other qualifications you need to be a top notch electrican. Between his excursions to football and the pub, he makes a very nice living around Tunbridge Wells and surrounding areas.

By now all us lads were on first name terms with the two Jocks, (Hamish and Rob) and supplying them with endless cups of tea and coffee from Joe's Diner. Hamish had gone over to his lorry and fetched his tool-kit, and soon the pair of them had Angus's transit engine stripped down in what seemed to me a hundred parts scattered and lying in Joe's Diner main car park. I thought to myself Hamish and Rob will never get the engine back together and working again! Soon, other truckers were joining our Scottish friends and everyone seemed to be telling each other how to repair the engine! I turned to the General and said, "Someone must know what they are up to," and the General filled me with confidence saying, "I doubt it, Trev!!"

"Fucking brilliant," I thought to myself!!! Just to make things even worse, it had now started to rain! We had arrived at the transport cafe at about eight or nine o'clock in the morning, and the time was now fast approaching midday.. Everyone was beginning to get a bit pissed off with the whole scenario! When all of a sudden, the engine was back together as quickly as it had been taken apart! Hamish told his mate Rob to turn the van's ignition key, NOTHING. "Try it again, Rob!" shouted Hamish. Still NOTHING, but then after about the fifth or sixth attempt, the sick transit burst into life. You would have thought Chelsea had just won a major cup-final, there was applause and congratulations and lots of back slapping. "She'll be okay now lads," Hamish and Rob informed us all! They started to walk back to their trucks. "Hold on a minute, men," I shouted to both Jocks, because while our two Scottish friends had been fixing Angus's rust-bucket, I had gone around to the rest of the heroes and had a whip-round. I managed to get about twenty pounds out of all the tight-arses, even Charlie and Spud Taylor had coughed up, which was most unlike them as you could never get a beer in a pub from these two likely lads. Twenty pound was a lot of money in those days! We were all very grateful to them, I even think Angus said a thank-you to the pair! Hamish and Rob, at first, would not accept our donation to the Scottish trucker's fund for stranded football hooligans, but in true Scottish style, quickly came around. After all our goodbyes we all piled into the trannie, and Hamish and Rob got into their trucks, they headed South and we started our journey north.

We had been delayed by about six hours, but we had plenty of time to spare, in actual fact we had still two days to spare, due to my mate dragging me out of The Roebuck on a Wednesday-cum Thursday morning, oh well such is life! Rubber-duck big-buddy, 10-4, and all that stuff, take me to the bright lights of Blackpool, please Mr Collins! And off we 'TRUCKED'. Our Yorkie-bars to the ready, and the open road ahead, I just hoped that Hamish and Rob had done a good repair job on trannie X, that the old girl would not let us all down again! Anyhow, it seemed okay for the moment, I told myself. I lent over and touched Angus' head with my hand touch wood!. After a few more miles along the road, one of our party asked me, "What was the problem with the engine?" According to our two Jock friends it was something to do with the manifold gasket sucking in air, and a couple of other things mechanical. I never really understood what the two Jocks were rabbiting about to me anyway, but that was as near an explanation as I could come up with. I tried explaining to Angus what had gone wrong with his old rust-bucket, but by this time he was lying flat out on the mattresses in the back of the van in the land of cans of Stella and Fosters. Mr Collins was still at the wheel of the trannie, and driving very nicely, without hitting too many bumps in the road. Now, Paul had missed a couple of seasons of following Chelsea, due to being on holiday. Her Majesty's pleasure, but we all make mistakes, don't we! It's just that when most people lose money at the bookies, that's it! We try again the next time to recoup our losses, we don't rob the bookie! But that said Paul and his brother Gary are both true-blues and really nice people when you get to know them! In fact, Gary was on this particular excursion as well as his brother, and had crashed out like a lot of the other heroes in the back of the trannie. The transit rattled along the motorway past Newport-Pagnell past the outskirts of Northampton and past Coventry. We must have gone around Birmingham's spaghetti-junction three or four times. One of the lads who was looking out of the window suddenly shouted out, "Look down there, Trev - Blackpool." I had to tell him to shut up, Blackpool, my foot! he was looking at Villa-Park, home of Aston-Villa football club. Finally, we managed to free ourselves from Birmingham and spaghetti-junction and headed off in the general direction of Sheffield, by-passing the towns of Derby and Nottingham, and joining up with the M62 motorway just outside Leeds. Then, the idea was to travel down the M62 across the Pennines skirting Manchester, before finally picking up the M55 into Blackpool! Well, that was the route we were planning to take, but as they say, the best laid plans of mice and men, and all that!

It had now been about five or six hours since our little escapade in Joe's Diner's car park, and everybody was beginning to get very peckish again so just outside Sheffield we drove into the motorway services to refuel the trannie and fill up on some grub. I think the services were called Woodall.

We all piled out of the transit and made our way to the food hall. We had to wait a little while for Angus to catch us all up, because now for about the first time since he had owned trannie x, he was locking it up, and closing the windows. "Did he know something that I didn't know," I asked myself. It was a bit late now looking after the old girl because for the last few years since he had owned it, I had never known him to lock it up. In fact, it was always left in The Roebuck car park with all its windows and doors left open, and he would let anyone use it. The only other conclusion for Angus's strange behaviour, was that perhaps he was thinking that now the engine had been repaired and fixed by our two Jock friends he would get a better price for it; or, on the other hand, was he thinking, that all people north of Watford are tea-leafs (thieves), and the trannie was too valued a commodity to be left unguarded. What I was left wondering was what does go through Angus's mind at times? Only one person in this world would know the answer to that, our darling and lovely Anna, Angus's beautiful wife. One day, I'll have a sit-down in the pub and have a serious talk about the meaning of life and the meaning of Angus with her, then perhaps not!!! Angus, by the way, when he was not terrorising, provoking and fighting with some rival fans, and when he was not in the pub, which was usually more often than not, earned his living from running about on industrial factory roofs as a sheeter. I will try to explain, to all you people who do not know, what a sheeter, otherwise known as an industrial-cladder, does. A sheeter is somebody who puts and fixes large metal sheets to newly erected large pre-formed steel buildings, and that in a nutshell is what a sheeter is, and Angus workwise was one of those. As were a lot of other people from Tunbridge Wells and the surrounding areas, for example: Mappe, alias Roger Mapp, in actual fact, I myself worked with Roger sheeting in of all places, Sadam-Hussein's 'IRAQ'. Mr Warren (Andy), Graham Haines (Ferret), Paul and Gary Collins, Scranner, Bobby Harbour and Mr Connie Butler Esq at some stage in their illustrious careers, have all carved a living for themselves from sheeting. What I can remember about sheeting was that it was bloody long hours and bloody hard work, but the financial rewards are quite good, (and if anyone tells you differently, then they have never done it, or else they are liars), and that is why a lot of people do it!

Meanwhile, back at the Woodall motorway services on the M1, everybody had been fed. A few of our party had managed to slip past the cashier on the food-till without paying. After an hour or so, it was once again time to set off for Blackpool. I was praying to myself that trannie x would start up without any trouble especially after what had happened the last time we had stopped. We all made our way back across the car park to where the transit was parked. It happened that four Ford transits had parked close to us. Inside them were United supporters travelling south for Leeds, Saturday match fixture in London. They had spotted that our trannie belonged to one of their most bitter and hated rival teams, Chelsea and had surrounded it like an Apache ambush. I think the rivalry between Chelsea and Leeds possibly started in 1970, when Chelsea beat them in the FA Cup Final, in the replay on the scum's patch, (Old Trafford.) In fact, I know it did! The Leeds supporters spotted some Union Jack banners with Chelsea written on them, that we were using as extra blankets for sleeping on in our trannie and put two and two together that some cockneys were about! They were just lying in wait for us, like a lion waits for its prey, but this time the prey was to be us, or was it?? I was at the front of our little group of warriors and alongside me stood the evergreen Paul Collins and his brother Gary, along with Bob Harbour and Ferret. Paul turned to me and said, "Fuck me, Trev. They're getting out of the vans!"

I had to think quickly! "How many do you reckon Paul?" I asked.

"Between 30 and 40," came the reply. By this time, all the Leeds United fans were out of their transits, and had started to bait us with cat-calls like, "You're going to get some, you Cockney bastards," and "this is where you die, you southern shit!" Nice dialogue! By this time we were only about 20 to 30 feet away from each other and outnumbered three or four to one! My brain was working overtime! Then, I remembered what Eccles had taught me, I quickly shouted to the rest of our group, "LINK ARMS AND FORM A LINE AND WALK TOWARDS THEM SLOWLY". The lads duly obliged, much to my amazement. My legs were turning to jelly now, us two warring factors were only about ten feet apart. Ferret wanted to steam straight into them! "WAIT!" I called, we were now within a body's length of each other, eye to eye contact indeed "CHELSEA," I shouted with all the air in my lungs, and pulled my arms away from my mate's as did the rest of our line. "DO THE NORTHERN SHIT," I was shouting, as I was kicking and punching at Leeds' fans. Some of the Leeds' fans had turned and run when they saw us walking towards them, which I had hoped would happen, because now we were much more evenly matched for a ruck. Good old Eccles, his tactics were certainly paying off. You could hear the sound of fists hitting faces, and the sound of boots hitting bodies, this was really toe-to-toe fighting at the raw end, and, for me what rucking and fighting is all about - the unexpected! The fighting was probably all over in about ten minutes, but when we relive the episode in the pubs and clubs back home and on the terraces, it went on for an hour, and there were one hundred Leeds' fans, not the thirty or forty! But these are the tales and stories that live on. After the car park fighting was over, and as often happens in these cases, a truce was called, the injured were picked up from the car park and helped to their respective transport. We headed north and they headed south. I think that Chelsea just won the day on points because we never bottled it in the ruck, and that's not being biased, it's just the way it was on the day, and neither Leeds or Chelsea lost face or terrace credibility at all after that result.

Back in the relative safety of Angus's trannie, stories were being told and swopped of who hit whom and some were already being blown out of proportion. I was just pleased that on this particular encounter no one was seriously injured or hospitalised, because, then, we would never have got to where we set out for, Blackpool. There was a lot of bruising and lumps and a few people had cuts about their persons, but there were no broken bones, thank God!

Let's not forget that other Godsend, Angus's trannie started FIRST TIME! Some years later, I was talking to Eccles and Sean in The Black Bull in the Fulham Road. We got on to the subject of Chelsea's past glories on the terraces, not on the field of play, that is! Eccles started telling me a tale about an almighty ruck between about a thousand Chelsea fans and the same number of Leeds United fans in Woodall service station, just outside Leeds on the M1. "What happened?" I asked.

"Well, Trev," replied Eccles, "apparently, Chelsea were going to a game in Blackpool, and Leeds were travelling in the other direction for a game." Eccles continued, "There was the old riot police attempting to break it up, and a lot of both Chelsea and Leeds fans were hospitalised that particular day. In fact, a couple of stabbings took place. They reckon the fighting lasted a couple of hours."

"When did that happen?" I asked Eccles. With that he told me the exact time and day of the alleged battle. "SP0T-ON," I thought to myself. Not wanting to dismay the great man's theory in anyway, I quickly made my way to the bar to get a round of drinks in. On returning to our table in the pub, Eccles and Sean were heavily in discussions about other serious matters. I placed the drinks on the table, and never said a word to Eccles about the Woodall-cum-Leeds affair. These sort of tales go from club to club and from terrace to terrace and get more and more unreal and exaggerated the more times they are told. Besides, the bobble-hat and woolly-scarf brigade thrive on stories such as these, it gives them a sense of street credibility . Even now up at the Bridge and in the surrounding pubs the Woodall incident is relived and told! I have often wondered to myself, if the Leeds' fans that were there that day tell a similar tale to their advantage in their pubs and clubs.

So now we were making our way across the Pennines, along the M62 and the route was going to take us skirting around Manchester to Chorley and up the M61 to Preston, before finally picking up the M55 into Blackpool - easy, WRONG! Somehow we had managed to take a detour off the M62 motorway and were heading for Blackburn and a place called Accrington, of Accrington-Stanley fame (an old football team). Fuck knows what we were doing going along this road, anyway, on further inspection of the map, our little detour wasn't going to matter that much, or lose us a lot of time on the journey, because we still had a day or so to get to Blackpool. And once we reached Blackburn or Accrington we could easily cut cross-country via Preston and into Blackpool. It was beginning to get near pub time and so we had a show of hands, which was it to be for the evening's stopover, Accrington or Blackburn? Accrington won the vote by eight to four, and so Accrington was the lucky town to have our patronage for the next twelve hours or more!

The next thing was to locate a half-decent pub, preferably, a pub where we could all kip down for the night. It did not look like we were going to have much luck. I turned to the General and said, "Perhaps we should have gone to Blackburn, this place is a one-horse town. No wonder their football team gave up the ghost! But who knows Garb, just perhaps?" We drove around Accrington for a while looking for a watering-hole, when I shouted to the General who was driving at the time to pull over. "What's up, Trev?" said the General to me.

"Garb," I replied, "I think I've just spotted Jonesey!!" Jonesey was a complete Chelsea nutter and loony, but had not been around on the terraces for a couple of years, due to being banged to rights by the Old Bill for such misdemeanours as using CS gas on rival supporters, (namely the Yids, Tottenham). Allegedly, he was also put in the frame for a stabbing, but this was never proved! As in Hickey's case, the Old Bill fabricated a lot of the evidence against him!

The trannie was parked up in a side street and we all got out and made our way to the pub where I thought I had seen Jonesey going into. As all us lads from the Well's walked into the pub, my eyes had not deceived me. There holding court to young Chelsea apprentices was, sure enough, Jonesey. I turned around to the General and said, "Garb the last time I saw that tosser was about five years ago on Chelsea's pre-season tour of Switzerland."

"Yeah, Trev I remember," said the General. With that, I gave a shout of "JONESEY, YOU WANKER." He nearly choked on his beer and without turning around and glancing towards me, shouted back, "T.D. YOU OLD TOSSER." We then turned and looked at each other, and it was as if it was slow-motion. I hadn't seen him for about five years but for the split second, time stood still for the pair of us old warriors. We could have been standing together rucking on the North-Bank at Highbury, or Tottenham's Park Lane, or anywhere in fact, it was a very nice moment for the pair of us, hooligan-cama-raderie, if you like! What followed, was a lot of back slapping, as if we were all long lost relatives and brothers. The drinking and the swopping of tales of terrace fights and battles continued until late into the night!

The landlord of the pub told us that if no one from our party caused any trouble, he would let us kip down in the back room bar. With that, I turned to Angus and Garb and said to the pair of them, we had got a right result. They both agreed. Besides, the landlord had taken a lot of money from us for drinks. I didn't want anyone walking the streets and getting nicked for being drunk and disorderly this close to the finishing-post.

Morning arrived, and it was a light breakfast in the pub before our final leg of the journey to Blackpool. We had a whip round for the landlord of the pub; found the transit; said our goodbyes to Jonesey; arranged to meet up with him at the game; had a quick head-count and off we all set to the tune of "Oh I do like to be beside the seaside."

We had been driving for a few hours, stopping off at various places to fill up on grub and booze, when suddenly there it was in the distance, the Blackpool Tower. A big cheer went up from everyone in the trannie. After all the aggro, we had made it! We drove along the Golden Mile. As it was only the afternoon and the football spe-cials were not due into Blackpool railway station until later, it was decided to get hold of a football from somewhere and have a kick-about on the beach and a paddle and a swim in the sea! We had found a large hotel-cum-pub and a large car park near the railway station. That was where we were planning to hole up in the evening, waiting for the rest of Chelsea to arrive on the specials; but for now it was football on the beach.

"We all mixed with the holiday makers, and soon found a large shop that sold footballs. In we all went, the poor young girl behind the counter just didn't know which way to look. We managed to throw the poor girl into complete and utter confusion, but we had got the result that we had hoped for and walked out of the shop with a couple of footballs. The General shouted, "Everyone on the beach." Like a load of loons and nutters we all piled onto the beach. It was a bloody hot day, as I recall, and some of the lads dived straight into the sea. We were joined on the beach by other small pockets of Chelsea fans, some, who like ourselves had made their way to sunny Blackpool by road, while others, had travelled up on the morning Intercity rattler from Euston. Beach-football quickly turned into a kick-about of about fifty people on each team and was beginning to get a little out of hand. It was decided to abandon the game and go for a walk along the Golden Mile and go into all the amusement arcades before finally settling into the boozer for a heavy evening's drinking session.

It was the usual crack in the arcades, everyone was trying to shake the machines and one-armed bandits to get the cash out of them and as we went from arcade to arcade we were being told to piss-off by the owners. We gave them back a barrage of verbal abuse. It was nothing too sinister, just piss-taking!! Then, of course, one of our little group had to take it a touch further! Mr Haines, alias Ferret, had been losing a few pounds to this certain machine, when the owner told him to stop shaking it. "Bollocks," came the reply!"

"Now, I've asked you to stop shaking my machine," said the arcade owner!"

"AND I'VE TOLD YOU, BOLLOCKS, NOW FUCK OFF, OUT OF IT," came Ferret's response!! "A red rag to a bull," I thought to myself. I turned to the General and Angus, the senior members of our little group, and said to them both, "Watch your backs lads, cause here we go again, FERRET'S JUST ABOUT TO LOSE IT. Before I could get out the words "lose it", ALL HELL BROKE LOOSE! Ferret head-butted the arcade owner right on the nose. BLOOD SPURTED EVERYWHERE. A few of the arcade owner's friends and helpers joined in, and a bloody battle occurred in the arcade. I knew the Old Bill would not be far away and would be soon on the scene, so we had to teach the enemy a lesson in manners very fast before plod could nick anyone of us Tunbridge Wells lads. The fighting could only have lasted five minutes before the sound of police sirens filled Blackpool air. About half a dozen Old Bill cars screeched to a halt outside the amusement-arcade. We had already lost ourselves, and were back on the beach mingling with the thousands of holiday makers. We were all watching the Old Bill lose themselves up their own arses and get into a state of right confusion, then we watched them get back into their little plod mobiles, and drive away. If only, they had realised their foe was watching them from only about two hundred yards away across the road. We all started to sing, "One-nil to Chelsea," over and over again.

We were now beginning to relax looking forward to the night's drinking session. Apparently the amusement arcade looked like the American bombing of Baghdad, with all the machines and bandits turned over, smashed and kicked in. It's surprising how much damage a few people can cause in the space of a very short time. Still, the way I looked at the whole episode was: Blackpool Old Bill - 0 Chelsea's away day 1.

The other moral of this particular tale is of course, don't upset a ferret because 'THEY HAVE A VERY NASTY HABIT OF BITING BACK.'

The following day, I picked up a local rag and there splashed across the front page with photographs of the damage caused to the arcade, were these headlines, 'THUGS AND HOOLIGANS, CAUSE FIVE THOUSAND POUNDS WORTH OF DAMAGE TO LOCAL AMUSEMENT ARCADE'. It went on to say that about two hundred rampaging Chelsea fans went berserk in this arcade and were all out of their heads on drugs and beer! 'WHAT A COMPLETE LOAD OF BULLSHIT - GOOD OLD BRITISH JOURNALISM AT ITS BEST,' I thought to myself, and, with that, I rolled the newspaper up into a ball and booted it as far as I could into the road! "The fucking best place for it," I told myself! MORE BAD PRESS FOR CHELSEA, and do we deserve it? NO, of course we don't!! More lies from the good old British Press. Still, when you have followed and witnessed the tabloid truths, (or should I say untruths) about Chelsea supporters as much as I have over the years, I suppose it is only what you must come to live with and expect. 'THE

FUCKING WANKERS', British Press that is!

The time was now fast approaching drinking time, so before we all got down to some serious heavy drinking in our newly found hotel-cum-pub, it was suggested that we try out some of the other pubs in the area we were in. The idea seemed to be harmless enough, OR SO I THOUGHT. Little did I realise that within the space of about one hour, I would be witnessing a mini riot.

We opened the main door to a pub and walked up to the bar to get served. It was a fairly large pub with one middle bar, which all us Chelsea fans were gathered in, and two other large bars, either side of the middle bar. We were now being followed around and joined by other members of the Chelsea family. I estimated we were now about one hundred, the Chelsea songs were now in full cry! Such classics as 'Hatchets and hammers, carving knifes and spanners, we'll show them West-Ham bastards how to fight, 'cos you won't take the Shed with the North-Stand in it, cos CHELSEA RULE ALRIGHT!' and "When Butch goes up to lift the F.A. Cup, we'll be there, WE'LL BE THERE!' Fuck knows why we always used to sing that one at every game, because it was rare for us to get very far in a cup run, in those days, but it was always a good moral booster. By the way, Butch was the nickname of the Chelsea captain of the day, (Ray Wilkins). Butch had two brothers who also played for the Blues, namely, Simon, who never featured much in first team action, and Graham, who was a defender. I use that term very loosely, because if you had ever seen Graham Wilkins play you would know exactly what I mean!! One particular classic moment comes to mind in the sparkling career of young Graham, it was a game down at the Dell, the then home of Southampton Football Club. I remember Graham hitting this back pass a fully thirty to forty yards past our bewildered and startled goalkeeper into his own net. We sank a few beers that night, I can tell you, and not in celebration!!! Paolo Maldini, the great Italian captain and defender - 'HE WAS NOT!!!' The last I heard about Mr Wilkins was that he was handling baggage at Heathrow, and that sentence just about sums up his career at Chelsea, baggage!! Anyhow, it was now, 'Knees up Mother Brown' time in the pub, and people were now standing on the tables, letting themselves go mental and pushing and shoving the person standing next to them. It was just a Chelsea fun thing and seen as no more than that! But it was good for Chelsea family bonding and camaraderie, and always would help to get you in the mood for any fighting or rucking to come! Us

Chelsea lads had taken over the pub. There must have been about two to three hundred of us packed into the place. Upon hearing the shouting and chanting, more and more pockets of Chelsea were coming through the main door and into the main bar of the pub.

I personally had not noticed anything strange, when all of a sudden Bob Harbour turned to me and said, "LOOK TREV," I looked around and said "BLOODY HELL BOB." In one of the other bars were about one-hundred Glasgow Rangers fans. It was a mass of blue and white. In the other bar to the other side of us were about the same number of green and white Celtic fans. Then somebody told me it was 'SCOTTISH-WEEKEND', where, apparently nearly all the crazies from Scotland come over the border to Blackpool and get pissed out of their heads for the entire weekend! It was a fire just waiting to be lit!! SMASH. Someone threw a bottle into the bar where the Celtic fans were. That was it!! The Celtic fans retaliated by throwing bottles and glasses at the Rangers fans. Chelsea were in the middle of it all. Rangers fans were coming through the bar we were in, to get at the Celtic fans, and the Celtic fans were trying to get through to the Rangers fans. It was fucking chaos, to say the least!! But not wanting to be outdone, the piss-head Chelsea brigade joined in, tables and chairs were broken up and used as weapons. The obligatory pool cues were used as spears and the pool balls were used for throwing at the enemy, whether they happened to be Chelsea Celtic, or Rangers fans.

The landlord and his staff were trying to get a grip of the whole situation. The optics behind the bars were smashed, because people were using them as a coconut-shy. The four large double-windows at the front of the pub were smashed . By this time the landlord of the pub had legged it. In seeing the landlord and his staff flee the premises, a few of the lads who were fighting saw a situation which they could turn to their advantage. They were straight behind the jump and nicking whatever wasn't damaged or smashed or broken. The pub tills were pushed down from the bars, opened up and rifled. I remember one Celtic fan in particular, coming at me, waving a pool cue above his head and shouting at the top of his voice, "HAVE SOME OF THIS! YOU COCKNEY WANKER!" I'd picked up a broken Cinzano bottle and was just going to smash him in the head with it when 'CRACK' a great shot by Andy Warren felled Mr Celtic. It hit the Jock in the side of the head like a missile, and he crumpled to the floor of the boozer, like a sack of shit! Blood spurted from his newly acquired head wound and I kept having flashbacks of Mel Gibson in the film 'BRAVE HEART'. By this time, there were injured bodies and blood everywhere.

The police sirens were getting louder and louder, so it was once again time for a quick exit! I shouted at the top of my voice, "COME ON CHELS, OLD BILL ARE HERE. EVERYONE OUT." With that cry most of the Chelsea disappeared through the now defunct windows and smashed doors of the pub, leaving the Celtic and Rangers fans to pick up the pieces from the carnage and have their collars felt by plod!!

Just as I was legging it from the boozer, I thanked Mr Warren for his good aim. I had one more duty to perform. I had to be quick though because plod were nearly on top of us now! I called to the General, who himself had blood running down the side of his face from a battle wound, to give me a hand. We got hold of Mr Celtic who by this time was still in the land of the fairies,, carried him from where he had been felled to one of the smashed windows and threw him through it onto the pavement and into the gutter. I turned to the General and with the Old Bill only a street away, said to him, "That's the best place for that Jock, in the gutter, let's lose ourselves and get your head wound sorted out!!" The General looked at me and said, "YEAH, TREV, CHEERS LET'S DO JUST THAT," and we were gone.

We made our way back to the home pub near the railway-station, which was only about a mile from the scene of the fighting that had just occurred, and all decided to keep our heads down for the rest of the evening, get all of the wounds patched up, and wait for the football-specials to arrive the following day! To me, it sounded like a fucking good idea. I looked around in our relatively quiet pub at all the faces, and came to the conclusion that all us Chelsea from Tunbridge Wells had seen enough action and enough of Blackpool for one day. We needed to rest a while for the battle and rucks to come. Besides, there wasn't a Celtic or Rangers fan in sight! THANK CHRIST!

I got chatting to the pub's landlady and she told me that if we didn't cause any trouble in her pub, she would find us all rooms for the night, which I thought was a right result. So I told the rest of the lads to be on their best behaviour, and we would have a bed for the night. It was now about one o'clock in the morning, and the only people in the bar were the landlady and I. She started to tell me how her old man had left her for a younger woman some years previous, and how she loved my cockney accent, then out of the blue she turned to me and said, "WELL, ARE YOU COMING TO BED THEN?" I thought to myself, you don't look a gift horse in the mouth and at least she's not a dog! I grabbed a bottle of scotch from behind the bar and followed her upstairs to her bedroom. I had a feeling I was going to be in for a long night with not too much sleep!

The morning finally arrived and all of us happy warriors were soon tucking into breakfast that the pub's staff had laid on for us. It was just a glorified fry-up of greasy bacon and eggs, etc, but it was grub, and we were all grateful for it, as we all needed to get some sustenance inside our healing bodies so that we were fit and at our best for the rigours of the day to come. I sat down at a table but I didn't feel like any grub. Also sitting around the breakfast table were good old Angus, Ian Cox, (the jockey) and Andy Warren. Angus turned to me and said, "Fuck me, Trev, what happened to you last night, then. You look completely SHAGGED OUT!" And with that observation from Angus, the entire Chelsea crew sitting down to breakfast burst out laughing and started taking the piss out of me, calling and shouting out things to me, such as, 'YOU LOOK LIKE YOU'VE BEEN COMPLETELY FUCKED, TREV! And 'DID SHE TAKE IT UP THE ARSE?' and other classic phrases! The word apparently was out that I had bedded the pub's landlady, so I just had to hold my hands up and take it on the chin! By this time the General had joined us at our breakfast table and wanted to know all the details of my conquest, so, of course, not being one to brag about such things, I had to tell him! Actually the landlady was a superb fuck and during the six or seven hours that I was with her, I had her three times, never up the arse, but she certainly taught me a thing or two about shagging, that was for sure.

Anyhow, it was now time to leave the pub and to make our way to the railway station to meet the rest of the Chelsea that would be arriving during the morning on the football specials from London. We all paid for our food and the previous night's sleeping arrangements and said our goodbyes and left the pub in one piece, and that was a miracle in itself. The pub's landlady was nowhere to be seen, so I said to Garb and Angus, that I would catch up with them in short while and that I had to find her so that I could thank her for all her hospitality and kindness she had shown to us Chelsea, and, of course, to ME!! I went back upstairs to the scene of the night before and opened the bedroom door and there she was, still lying stark naked on the large double bed. I leant over and kissed her and said to her, "Bye then," to which she replied, "Bye! and have a good match, and if you're ever up in Blackpool again"!! But we both knew in our heart of hearts that would never be the case, but I still had to give her one last passing shot, so I took a swig of whisky from the bottle that we had taken to bed with us the previous night; and to take a phrase from the lads at breakfast time about did she take it up the arse. I COULD NOW TELL THEM THAT SHE DID!

I later caught up with the rest of the lads and the General turned to me and said, "You're nothing but a randy old man, Trev!" to which my reply was, "If it's on a plate and staring you in the face, Garb, then take it!!" "POINT TAKEN, TREV," said the General to me. We then opened up a couple of cans of lager and toasted to all of our latest successes, rucks, and in my particular case, CONQUEST! The football specials finally arrived at the station and the train's carriage doors all burst open to the cries of, "CHELSEA BOYS WE ARE HERE, SHAG YOUR WOMEN, AND DRINK YOUR BEER," over and over again! Of course that had all ready been done! There was a lot of back-slapping and greeting of each other as if we hadn't seen each other for years, when we had all been drinking together and standing in the SHED at Chelsea just a few days earlier! All us Tunbridge Wells Chels marched to Blackpool's ground with about a hundred other Chelsea fans who had just got off the specials. We were by now in full voice singing Chelsea songs and calling out battle cries. By now, there was a heavy police presence all around us, and the usual crack of some Old Bill on mounted horse-back. This was just to make sure that nobody caused any trouble en route, which was furthest from any of our minds. 'OF COURSE'!

We arrived at the ground at about one o'clock which was a couple of hours before the game was due to kick-off. We were now joined by hundreds and hundreds of other Chelsea, all mingling about just outside Blackpool's home end. The gates opened early as I recall, and all us Tunbridge Wells Chelsea and about two hundred other members of the Chelsea family put on our best northern accents to gain entry to their end. Once inside the ground, there was not much to do, there weren't any bars, so we just had to wait for the Blackpool fans to show up for the fun to begin! By this time, a lot more Chelsea from the specials had joined us in the Blackpool end and most of the faces recognised each other through winks and grins! As being Chelsea, we didn't talk or speak to each other because that would have taken away the element of surprise; and the Blackpool fans would have quickly sussed that we were in their end mingling with them. By now the Blackpool fans were turning up in their hundreds onto their home terrace and were starting to take the piss out of all the travelling Chelsea, who had just arrived on the specials, quite unaware that standing with them were about three hundred of Chelsea's most wanted! The Blackpool fans continued to shout abuse, only because there was a large fence and a thin blue line of Blackpool's finest protecting them, or else, I don't think they would have been so brave! Anyhow, it wasn't going to matter much very shortly, because they were soon to get the hiding of their northern lives! ENOUGH was ENOUGH, no more abusing our Cockney brothers. The cries went up! "CHELSEA HERE, CHELSEA THERE, CHELSEA EVERY FUCKING WHERE," and "YOU'RE GOING TO GET YOUR FUCKING HEADS KICKED IN." Before the Blackpool fans and the Old Bill realised what was happening, we were into them, much to the delight of all the Chelsea fans who were parked behind the fence, and were now applauding our efforts with Chelsea battle cry hymns. The boots and fists were flying into the unsuspecting Blackpoolers from each and every direction, and they were falling like flies and fleeing to the safety of the police and the turnstiles. All us Chelsea stood on the Blackpool home terrace and milked the applause! It was as if we were Roman Gladiators who had just won a great victory! In fact, whenever, Chelsea took a home end at any away ground, it always made me feel special and PROUD!! The Old Bill by this time had finally worked out what had just happened and had mustered up reinforcements and were now in the process of escorting all us heroes to the terrace, where all the other travelling Chelsea fans were. We had done what we had set out to do and that was to take Blackpool's home end. When we finally got to our new found home, I turned to the General who by this time was standing beside me and said, "Garb, there seems to be a lot of green and white about on the terraces here with us?" To which the General replied, "YEAH, TREV, THEY'RE ALL CELTIC FANS, and are joining with us today to fight BLACKPOOL and RANGERS fans." Then I looked up at the terrace that we had taken only about an hour earlier and noticed that the Old Bill were letting Blackpool fans back onto it, I also noticed that with the Blackpool fans were Ranger fans. I turned back to the General and said, "GARB MATE, I NOW SEE WHAT YOU

MEAN!!" Before I could finish my sentence, there was a hail of smashing glasses and bottles and bricks being thrown and hurled through the air at us all! Some of the Chelsea and Celtic fans were getting hit and falling to the ground with head wounds, there was blood and people crying out in pain everywhere. We were all easy targets as we were packed into the one-sided terrace like sardines, and the fucking Old Bill wouldn't let us back out of the terrace for safety reasons! So we just had to take the bottling the best we could until plod decided we had had enough punishment for one day and got amongst the Blackpool and Rangers supporters to break it up. It must have carried on for at least ten minutes. Two thousand football crazies can throw an awful lot of bottles, glasses, lumps of concrete and bricks in that short space of time!

When the game finally finished the Old Bill let all of us Chelsea and Celtic fans out of our locked up sheep-pens that Blackpool called a terrace enclosure and back onto the streets. We didn't have to wait too long to be confronted by the Blackpool and Rangers fans, simply because Blackpools' 'FINEST' had only gone and let the Blackpool and Rangers fans out onto the streets at the same time AS US! Talk about brains! Perhaps they wanted another riot on their hands be-cause that is what they were just about to get again! You could never have imagined the Fulham Old Bill letting the away fans at the Bridge out of the ground at the same time as us Chelsea - we would have murdered them! Admittedly, on occasions we used to wait for them in the near vicinity of the ground to give them a fucking good hiding and a kicking, but at least the Fulham Old Bill used to keep the away fans in the ground for any time up until an hour and only let them out of the ground when they thought it was safe to do so!

But this wasn't the case with Blackpool's finest. WE WERE ALL OUTSIDE ON THE STREETS TOGETHER (CHELSEA AND CELTIC v BLACKPOOL and RANGERS fans, a time-bomb just waiting to EXPLODE!! You could sense it in the air, the feeling of pent-up emotions, hatred and evil aggression! The Old Bill were keeping a low profile by now, and were nowhere to be seen! I per-sonally think that they wanted a blood-bath on their hands! All the warring parties found a large piece of wasteland, which just hap-pened to be near where we had parked up Trannie X for safe-keep-ing. For a short while we just stood staring at each other.

There must have been about a thousand Rangers and Blackpool fans grouped together and about the same number of us Celtic and

Chelsea fans - then it went off, BIG TIME. Both sets of us nutters and fans launched and ran at teach other with blood curdling screams and shouts. It was now just a question of who wanted it the most, THEM OR US! I could see a lot of the Rangers and Blackpool fans had picked up lumps of wood, bricks, broken beer bottles and glasses to hit us with. I was standing with the General, Match, Ian Cox, (Bimbo), Ferret and Bobby Harbour and somehow through all the chaos and aggro had also been joined by our old mate from our overnight stay in Accrington, Jonesey and all of his merry men! By this time I was going completely mental and charging like some sort of wild animal at the enemy! I had a broken cider bottle that I was holding and gripping tightly in my hand and letting out a heart stopping cry of, "CHELSEA" and "HAVE SOME OF THIS, YOU NORTHERN FUCK PIG'S." I smacked the first Blackpool Rangers fan I could get to - as it happens I struck lucky with my opening flurry of punches and hits, and caught two of the enemy with one blow of the cider-bottle! Blood spurted from a head wound and as the cider bottle glanced off the side of his head, it caught another Blackpool Rangers fan also in the head, they both hit the deck like shit and the boots went in!! It was close-counter stuff and rucking at its best. People were falling all around I was in my element, fighting at football with your mates by your side, what could be better! Then I felt something strike me on the back of my head and it wasn't good! I immediately put my hands up to hold my head and blood poured through my fingers like someone had just turned on a water tap I HAD BEEN HIT. The last thing I can remember was crumbling to the ground and completely blacking out.

The General came with me to the hospital. I remember the ambulance men asking me if I was a Celtic fan, because someone had got a green and white Celtic scarf and wrapped it around my head to try to stop the flow of blood from my wound. Garb informs me that I kindly told the ambulance men to, "GET FUCKED", and that I was Chelsea before blacking out for the second time. Apparently, I had been felled by half a house brick and had lost a lot of blood. The nurse at the hospital said I was lucky to be alive. How true that was, I don't know, I needed twenty stitches in my head and was walking around like an Egyptian mummy for months afterwards. I had a lump on the back of my head the size of a cricket ball. Still, the way I look at it is, IF YOU LIVE BY THE SWORD, YOU ALSO DIE BY THE SWORD. On this occasion, that was nearly the case. Thank the Lord for ambulance men, nurses, hospitals, and mates!! Blackpool's main hospital that day looked like a scene from the television programme 'MASH' with ambulances picking up the injured and bringing them into the hospital to be inspected by the doctors and nurses. There were Chelsea, Celtic, Blackpool and Rangers fans all mingling together in the hospital corridors and wards. The recent fighting was put on hold while the injured had their broken bones and war wounds fixed and their cuts stitched.

The doctors told the General that I would have to stay in hospital overnight. When the General told me that, I said, "FUCK THAT, GARB, COME ON WE'RE OFF!" With that I got up and proceeded to walk out along the long corridors of the hospital. The nurses were trying to stop me leaving and advising the General that I should at least stay in overnight for observation. All I wanted to do was get back to where we had parked Trannie X and crash out on the mattresses in the back. I had certainly had enough of Blackpool for one day and couldn't wait to see good old Tunbridge Wells and especially THE ROEBUCK once again.

As myself and the General were about to step outside the hospital's main doors, I saw that the ambulances were still bringing in the injured fans, and I noticed a couple of walking wounded leaving an ambulance, they were both Rangers fans. Well, at least they were wearing Rangers shirts! On seeing this, I had a flashback to the events of earlier and flew into one. I had forgotten about my own injuries and was punching and kicking out at them. The ambulance men, nurses and doctors ran over to break it up. Garb, the General, had by this time, grabbed hold of me and was dragging me away once again from the enemy, but I had still managed to land a few good kicks and punches. I remember the doctors and ambulance men shouting at the General TO GET THE LITTLE FUCKER OUT OF IT. According to the General, I collapsed in a heap on the ground once again, Garb, with the help of a couple of Celtic fans, carried me to Angus's trannie and laid me in the back of it for the journey back to Tunbridge Wells. The next thing I remember is Bobby Harbour and Match waking me up to tell me that I had been to sleep for nearly 24 hours and that we were only about 15 miles from our home town.

It had taken a day to travel back from Blackpool to Tunbridge Wells and on the way back home, the lads had pulled up in a lorry park and helped themselves to the contents of a beer lorry. In the back of the trannie were a dozen crates of beer and in each crate there were 36 bottles. This was in the days of lorries having canvas which meant that you could lift up the canvas sheeting and have a look to see what was there. In this case, the lads had came up TRUMPS. My head was still bloody sore. It felt like Ringo was inside my head banging his drum-kit but the free beer was going to flow in The Roebuck when we all got back to H.Q. that night, that was for sure. And so, the trip to sunny Blackpool was completed, all of us heroes had returned home safely once again, battered and injured, but the wounds would soon heal. The Blackpool trip would be relived on the terraces and pubs around Stamford Bridge and SW6 for a good many years to come and none more so than in The Roebuck public house in Royal Tunbridge Wells.

Another game that sticks in my mind was an evening encounter up at Bramell Lane, home of Sheffield United. Myself, the General, Ian Cox, Angus, Bob Harbour, Match and Bob Desautels and Andy Warren had all travelled up north on a British Rail football special, and, as I recall, it was fucking freezing. The heaters on the rattler were not working and the windows in our carriage were all broken, but this was normal for good old British Rail football-specials. We were treated like animals going to market to be killed! In fact cattle are probably treated with more respect, in fact I know they are!! Still it was only what us Chels had come to expect from British Rail's rolling stock - total crap and this was the middle of winter, December, with snow falling. As the train hurtled along the track on its journey north, the icy cold wind circled around our carriage at about 70-80 miles per hour, at least we had managed to stock up on whisky before we left London, so at least that helped to keep the cold out a little bit. By this time, we were about halfway to Sheffield, and the next thing I knew was the door to our carriage being opened, and there standing like some Army General before us was Eccles, the undisputed leader of Chelsea's hard-core and the No.1 face at the Bridge. "What the fuck are you Tunbridge Wells up to?" he asked, "you won't be in any fit state for the ruck in Sheffield, freezing your bollocks off in this poxy carriage. Come into mine. Babs and Sean are in my carriage further down the train"

Fuck me, we didn't have to be asked twice, what an honour to be asked to sit with Babs, Sean and Eccles. It was to us lads as if John Lennon had just walked up to us and invited us to sit with him, Paul, George, and Ringo. The trip was turning out to be not so bad after all, I told myself!!

Upon sitting with Babs, Sean and Eccles in their carriage, all us
Tunbridge Wells lads were presented with photocopies of drawings
of Sheffield United's ground. On the drawings were arrows pointing
to certain places where Eccles wanted us lads to meet up. He also
told us all to make our way to the ground in ones and twos. This way,
he explained, we would be able to infiltrate the home end without the
Old Bill suspecting anything was wrong. A cunning plan indeed and a
typical Eccles' manoeuvre. The rest of Eccles' entourage were, by
now, distributing the same drawings up and down the rattler (train) to
the rest of the travelling Chelsea so everyone knew what to do once
we arrived in Sheffield!

The train pulled into Sheffield and the carriage doors opened as
one to the old Chelsea battle cry of 'CHELSEA BOYS WE ARE
HERE, SHAG YOUR WOMEN, AND DRINK YOUR BEER,'
over and over and over again! The Old Bill were waiting to escort us
to the ground on mounted horseback. The non-fighters went with
them but all the rest of us Chels made our own way to the ground in
dribs and drabs, as Eccles had told us to do. We went to the home
end. As I looked around at the faces surrounding me on the terracing
I saw familiar faces from the train and others that I recognised as
London Chelsea. Everyone had their scarves hidden inside their donkey jackets, waiting for the cry of "CHELSEA" to go up from Babs
or Eccles, the sign to run the Northerners from their home end and
to give them a fucking good hammering!! We did not have to wait
long for the cry to come, kick-off for the game was scheduled for 8
o'clock and about a quarter to eight the cry went up and echoed
through the cold December night's air. The Chelsea scarves were out
and all hell was taking place. I remember that I was standing next to
Bob Harbour and Angus that night, and Angus, still quite pissed, saying, "COME ON TREV, WE'RE CHELSEA, KAMIKAZE, CHEL-
SEA," and with that he ran and jumped right on top of one of the
Sheffield fans who by this time were running for their lives. We were
now all lashing out and putting the boot into anyone wearing red and
white Sheffield United's colours. The United fans poured onto the
pitch side, looking for police protection, and they got it from the
northern bill, but not before they had all got a fucking good kicking
and beating. The fighting was over in about 5 minutes and the Sheffield home end had been taken. Eccles, planning had worked well
and yet another job WELL DONE by the master!

The rest of the evening was spent watching the match with a cor-

don of Sheffield's finest thin blue line around us, but the victory was
so easy and so sweet, the Northerners just could not believe it. They
were by now all sitting around the side of the pitch on the running
track and the rest of them were sitting in other parts of the ground.
They were really pissed off, especially when they looked up at us
Chelsea fans taking the piss out of them all, and particularly when they
realised their home end of about six thousand strong Blade fans (Sheffield United fans) had been taken by only about three to four hundred
Chelsea fans - a major victory for all us conquering heroes indeed!

On the way home that evening, I remember Eccles and Babs walking along the train and going into each and every carriage on the rattler
congratulating his men, or as Eccles put it, his troops, oh yes, and he
was also collecting donations, which, he told us would go towards
paying British Rail for any damage anyone had done to the train and
to help pay for any fines anyone had picked up from any previous
rucks the week before! Personally, I never knew whether Eccles was
being genuine about paying for fines  and paying for any damage
caused to good old British Rail football-specials. Of course, nobody
in their right minds was going to ask him about it anyway. So everyone on the away day special trains used to hand over any amount of
loose change that they had in their pockets up to say a £1 in those
days. That may not seem a lot of money, but when you have got
anything from four to eight hundred Chelsea travelling together to an
away game every couple of weeks throughout the football season, it
works out as a lot. The general opinion was that the whip rounds
were to pay for EABHA, which stood for 'Eccles and Bab's holidays
abroad', I never believed that rumour, as I had, on many occasions,
bumped into the great man at Horseferry Magistrates Court or
Marylebone Magistrates Court, when I was paying my own fines for
such misdemeanours as causing an affray, breach of the peace and the
old favourite GBH, of which I was totally innocent!

It was so cold that December night up in Sheffield, that I recall
going up to a hotdog seller. Gathered around his stall were about
thirty other Chelsea fans ordering a dozen hotdogs, a dozen hamburgers and meat pies and I passed the food back behind me to all
and sundry who were standing there with me at the time. The hotdog
vendor must have thought he had a right result with those, greedy
Chelsea fans! WRONG! "Oh yeah, I'll have ten No 6, as well, please."
(which were the cigarettes of the day). As the northern twat bent
down and turned to give me the fags and before he could tally up the

amount I owed him for the grub, I was gone. I knew the hotdog bloke would not come after me, as the rest of the Chelsea, that were gathered around his stall, would have only too happily relieved him of his hard-earned takings without too much fuss and bother!! Honest folk, us Chelsea fans, no we really are!!! We were putting our fingers into the hot cups of Bovril to keep our hands warm it was that fucking cold, but such is life!

Years later we all went to Tromso to watch the heroes play and if I had thought that Sheffield was a little bit on the chilly side, it was the Caribbean compared to this shithole, I thought I was a fucking Snowman. Tromso is only about 200 miles inside the Artic Circle, in fact Tromso is the most northern professional football club anywhere in the world. I looked at the General (Garb), Angus, Match and Charlie from Tunbridge Wells and said, "How the fuck, can they play football in these conditions!" It was snowing so badly you could only see about 15 to 20 yards ahead. Then, just when you told yourself things couldn't get any worse, it did!! There was a fucking great blizzard and it snowed and snowed and SNOWED!! The General turned to me and said, "I know how we can keep warm, Trev. Let's go and smack a few Norwegians and run them from the terraces."

"Yeah, a great idea, Garb," I replied, "but there's just one slight problem with that."

"What's that?" asked the General.

"Well Garb, WHERE are the TERRACES?" Because they were unrecognisable under the masses of snow, "And I can't see any Norwegians up for a ruck, can you, Garb?"

"Point taken, Trev!" We opened up another bottle of Jack Daniels and soon forgot about the farce!

I can remember walking up to the tiny Alfhein Stadium, and looking at the cars that were parked in the small car park and they were buried in snow. Once inside the ground, the mounds of snow were as high as the goal's crossbars and it was still SNOWING!! The game itself was a joke, a complete load of bollocks and I could not wait to get on the plane home! I love my trips abroad but this place was shit!! Just for the record we lost the game 3-2, but I was not concerned about the score because I knew that in a fortnight's time, with the second leg to be played on grass at the Bridge, Chels would thrash the Norwegian no hopers and it was the case! Chelsea 7, Tromso 1, aggregate 9-4, a hat-trick and the match ball for VIALLI, do you remember him, Ken? When will you ever learn?

The nearest we got to a ruck in Tromso was a huge snowball fight with the airport personnel before our flight back to good old Blighty. So that was Tromso and was I glad to take off from that airport. The plane landed back at Gatwick and as we bounced comfortably onto the runway, a burst of applause broke out from the travelling Chelsea fans on the plane. I think we were all relived to be back home. I have come to the conclusion that Norway is only fit for reindeer and men in long, white beards, come to think of it, don't I know someone that fits that description?! Surely Tromso could do with a new chairman, they must need one!! please!!! Oh well, we live in hope.

# CHAPTER 3

## LUTON

By this time, all us hooligans were proven travellers. Whether travelling by train or transit vans we were always there, supporting and fighting for our team. Chelsea fans used to turn up at grounds in their thousands and the night Chelsea played Luton, it was being televised on BBC1. I remember Chelsea scoring and about five thousand Chelsea fans went and fought any Luton fans they could find. The cameras were straight on us, nationwide coverage and great for our reputation as No.1 thugs. But Chelsea were supposed to be banned, weren't we? Surely good old Dennis Howell had put a ban on us? But how could the Old Bill, let five to ten thousand Chelsea fans roam Luton town centre? What they did was let us all into the game, so they could keep an eye on us. Big mistake that!!

Then after the game we were herded back to Luton railway station like animals, being beaten about the head by police on horseback with batons. We were put on trains back to London with minimum damage done to Luton that night and as Chelsea had won the match, everyone was fairly happy. But Luton Town is the pits, a right shithole of a ground. Next time Chelsea went there, the story was completely different. I remember Luton officials had a great idea of employing stewards who would keep fans under control and chuck out troublemakers and thugs. They wore pink coats. I think the idea was because the colour was neutral and wouldn't upset anyone - wrong! It was like a red rag to a bull, the police would just act as backup. When the stewards in pink coats (the Pink Panthers) started throwing out Chelsea fans, the head-hunters and other Chelsea fans went berserk, murdering all the stewards they could lay their hands on and fighting on the pitch.

After the match, the police tried to escort us back to the railway station, but we all broke rank and went on the rampage, causing mass destruction in the town centre. To be nicked by Plod is one thing, that was fair game, but to have dickheads in pink coats acting as police was a completely different ball game and totally unacceptable to Chelsea. I was with Mappe (Roger Mapp) another Roebuck legend that night, also the General, Match and Andy Warren. Suddenly, as we turned a corner, about fifty Luton fans came at us from nowhere, hitting us with iron bars and bricks and pickaxe handles. We didn't run, we had to take it, Chelsea never bottled it! There didn't appear to be anymore Chelsea anywhere to help us. I thought to myself, "This is it, hospital or morgue, this is where we get killed." the General picked up a metal dustbin lid and said, "Have this, you Luton bastards" and downed about three of them. Blood spurted from one of the Luton fan's heads and the Luton lads backed off a bit. The General then picked the lid up again and hurled it through a shop window, smashing the glass, I thought to myself, "What the hell is he doing. It was an iron-mongers shop; tools and lots of things to use for fighting. "Help yourself lads," the General said, and before Luton could come at us again we were all tooled up, although heavily outnumbered. A bit like John Wayne's film 'The Alamo'. Luton came at us again, but this time we were armed. I had managed to nick a crowbar, so had Match - Crunch! - right across a couple of Luton fans backs. Chelsea were fighting back. I then saw Match laying into Luton like a loonie. Mappe and Andy were joining in the fun with hammers and broom handles and anything else that they could get from the ironmongers.

Luton fans were lying in the gutter, blood everywhere. Although a couple of us got a good kicking and a few broken bones, we had won the night. Luton fled. I think Andy got a broken leg that night and I fractured my arm, but we carried Andy back to the railway station. There was Claret (blood) everywhere, and our reputation was growing by the minute. I remember celebrating that night. The General still with his dustbin lid threw it through an off licence window. Someone shouted, "Help yourselves." Suddenly, about one hundred Chelsea fans appeared and helped us to kick the plate glass window in. Everyone was helping themselves to free wines, beers and spirits. Where did all the other fans appear from? They hadn't been around five minutes ago when we were fighting for our lives. I grabbed a bottle of Scotch that would do nicely to relieve the pain, when, suddenly, we heard the police sirens. Everyone scarpered, but not before I had picked up a few more bottles of vodka and Cinzano, my favourite tipple.

Back at Luton railway station, Chelsea were in their thousands. The plod were not concerned about us, they just wanted to get us out of Luton as quickly as possible, which they did by putting on extra trains to take us back to London. How the Old Bill hated Chelsea. I shall never forget that journey back to London. Halfway back, everyone was relaxed after a good night's fighting, drinking and getting stoned. Suddenly there was a strong smell of burning. Smoke started appearing in the carriages. "Bloody hell!" said the General, "Some prat has set the fucking train alight."

"Fuck off," I said to Garb, "I don't feel very well, and I'm trying to kip."

"No it's for real," said Garb. I still thought he was joking, but the next thing I knew, the General and Andy had got hold of me and carried me off the train, which by this time had stopped in the middle of the countryside, as flames were coming from the carriages. "Are all Tunbridge Wells here?" Garb asked. We had a quick head count.

"No," said Mappe, "Match is missing."

"Fuck me!" said the General," we've got to find him. Who saw him last?" Angus said that he had been playing cards with Match in the guards van at the back of the train, but we didn't know whether to believe him or not, as he was pissed out of his mind as usual! The first three carriages of the train were really on fire by now, and there were only two carriages left before the smoke and flames reached the guards van. Garb, Mappe and Andy went over to look for Match, whilst Angus and I and a few hundred others lay in the damp grass, being very ill.

When Mappe, Andy, and Garb reached the guards van they all started shouting and banging on the side of it, "Match are you in there? the fucking train's on fire. GET OUT!!" There was still no reply coming from the burning train. By this time, the night air was filled with smoke. We were all concerned as to Match's whereabouts.

Then, the guard's door slowly opened and there stood Match, trousers around his ankles, and saying, "What's all the fuss about? I'm halfway through a bunk-up!" The little sod had been shagging a bird in the empty guard's van, and didn't even know the train had caught fire. In fact, Match thought we were back in London. So, before the train was completely gutted we got Match and the naked bird out safely. The bird's name eludes me, but then they all did in those days, they were just fair game. If they travelled with us for a shag, that was it, no long term relationships - women had no place in football.

The train finally burnt out completely. There must have been about one thousand Chelsea lads standing on the grass watching it burn. It certainly got a tremendous cheer! British Rail laid on another train to get us back home to London, which was very good of them, considering what we had done to the first one. We all used to travel without tickets, the usual way, was to wait until the train was about to pull out of the station, and then you would jump on. Everyone knew how to work it, this was called 'jibbing'. If a 'Hector' (ticket inspector) came along, the best move was to all cram into the bog on the train until he went, or if he was annoying - a bad old Hector, we would have a whip round amongst the people who looked like they had a few quid and bribe him with the proceeds. That always seemed to work! Nowadays, it's a football shirt for his kid that seems to do the trick.

That wasn't the only situation when money was needed from fellow supporters on the rattlers. Other occasions were when another fan had been nicked by the Old Bill at the previous week's game and had a Court appearance pending, which usually meant a fine. In this case, everyone on the train would dig deep into their pockets for some loose change to help pay the fine. So, it didn't really matter if you got nicked, there were always ways to get around things and your mates would always help you out.

Mappe (Roger Mapp) was born of Caribbean parents and his spiritual home was Barbados where his father was a police officer. I have known Mappe ever since I was knee-high. He has always been one of the lads - built like a brick shit-house and as hard as nails. You could liken Roger to a young Mike Tyson or Mumhammad Ali. He used to be a bouncer in the local nightclubs in Tunbridge Wells, Chez Moi and the Elizabethan Barn. He also used to do a bit of amateur boxing. He was also a doorman in the local pubs, keeping the riff-raff out and giving the young 'uns a quick clip round the ears and sending them home to mummy for an early night. I worked with Mappe in Baghdad, Iraq in 1984, and we shared digs together. He is a great ladies' man, is Rog, but also a gentleman and one of the nicest people you could wish to meet. If you upset him, you did so at your own peril! Mappe loved football and loved Chelsea, and more than that he loved the fighting on the terraces. Roger was once going out with the daughter of somebody important in the local police. When her dad found out who Mappe was, he decided that it would be better for his daughter not to see him anymore and said to Mappe, "All you soccer thugs should be kicked in the bollocks and have your arms and legs cut off. You're not seeing my daughter again, so fuck off." Nice language for a police officer!

I suppose it's just the sort of language you would come to expect of the Old Bill. In a lot of respects there's not a lot of difference between them and us. Seeing as though Mappe's old man was a police officer in Barbados' finest, you might have thought some sort of bonding would have taken place, but no! Nevertheless, not being one to be put off by a prattish threat like this, Mappe carried on seeing her and amazingly the copper became fond of him but that was Mappe, and still is. God bless him!

Andy Warren, a complete and utter Chelsea nutter, was one of the first people I ever 'jibbed' a train with - the occasion was a second division match, Cardiff were at home to Chelsea. Ninian Park was Cardiff City's home ground and Andy, myself, Pete Jefferys and Coxy decided to leave The Roebuck at midnight after another night of heavy drinking and pill popping. We decided to 'thumb it' and 'jib' the rattlers to Wales. The General, Match, Mappe, Hickey and a few others were travelling down to Cardiff by transit. Why the fuck we didn't, I shall never know. As we all fell out of the pub, I remember saying to the General, "See you in Wales in the morning." It seemed like a good idea at the time - another big mistake! The General's reply was, "Fuck off! You'll never make it all the time you've got a hole in your arse, Trev!" The challenge was down, that was it, off we set into the dark night. We managed to get a lift to London on a fruit and veg lorry on its way to Covent Garden. Once in London, we made our way to Paddington to 'jib' the intercity train to Cardiff. It was 3am and it had only taken us three hours to get from Tunbridge Wells to Paddington - not bad going for four pissed up football fans! When we got to Paddington there were thousands of Chelsea fans just mincing about. The rattler was due to leave at 5am. Great! I had thought that we would be in Cardiff by at least 10 o'clock in the morning. Plenty of time to get pissed in the local pubs and go on the rampage down there. "Time to kip," I said to Andy but he was already shoving Coke up his nose like it was going out of fashion. I remember saying to Andy, before I cuddled up next to some old slag, that one day he would blow his nose into orbit but Andy being Andy didn't give a fuck as usual!

Next thing I knew, I felt a kick in my back, it was Coxy. "Wake up, Trev, the rattler's in. I quickly came to my senses, kissed the old slapper goodbye, promised I would see her again (fat chance!) and off we all set, with all the other milling Chelsea to 'jib' the train. British Transport Police were everywhere. "Tickets please!" was the cry. 'Oh yeah!' we all thought, and about two to three hundred fans approached the ticket turnstile. There were about three guards, as some fans had tickets and the guards were checking these, it was easy to slip past unnoticed - no problem! All four of us had made it and we were on the train. The transport police didn't seem to mind, I think they just wanted to go home to bed! They always seemed to turn a blind eye where Chelsea fans were concerned.

The train set off, and I thought I would settle down and get some sleep, after sorting out the slag I was knackered. I couldn't wait to meet the General in Wales and tell him what a good trip we had had. How wrong I was to be! The train stopped at Reading, why, I don't know, but Mr Warren woke me up. "Fuck off Andy!" was my reply.

"No, Trev we've got to change trains," he insisted. So off we got, still half asleep, along with a few others who thought we knew what we were doing! We were standing by the train when it suddenly pulled away leaving us standing, unable to get back on either from being too pissed or too tired and we watched it disappear into the night. A few Chelsea lads made it back on, but not Andy and I, we were left watching the back of the train, like a couple of local dickheads! I turned to Andy and said, "You fucking wanker! What are we going to do now, standing in the middle of nowhere in the middle of the night?"

"No problem, Trev," says Andy "I used to live here. I know the area we'll jib another train."

I said to him, "Fuck me Andy, they ain't like buses - miss one and another one comes along in another minute!"

"No sweat, Trev," he replied "there's a station not far from here." So off we set, walking down the track and across fields to Andy's station! I later found out that the only reason the train had stopped was because some prat had pulled the emergency cord, so we could have both stayed on the train and gone straight through to Cardiff, which seemed by now a very, very long way away indeed, as we continued our marathon walk.

Coxy and Pete J (Butcher) will be dreaming of a good ruck to-morrow with those Welsh sheep shaggers in a nice warm carriage, and here I am freezing my bollocks off with my old coke mate Andy. What a tosser I am!!!! I asked Andy where the railway station was and all he said was "There's one round here somewhere, I used to live in this area."

"Where the fuck is it, Andy?" I said. By this time, we must have walked 5 miles or more and it was beginning to get light. Then we saw a road, which led to the M4, that meant Wales, so thumbs out hoping for a lift, but to no avail. We made the Severn Bridge into Wales at five o'clock in the evening. The match had finished by then, so all we could do was turn around and make our way back to London. I was not happy with Andy that day, so we just waited in the motorway services for a lift back to 'the smoke' and home. As it happened, it wasn't too long before we got a lift, as a lot of Chelsea were coming back after the game. I happened to spot a couple of lads I knew from Brixton, Charlie and Finney, a great couple of fighters, who had room for a couple of waifs and strays in their mini. So, at last, we could get back to London in comfort. I told Charlie and Finney our story. After they had finished pissing themselves with laughter we set off home.

Brixton Charlie and Finney were Shedites and knew all us Tunbridge Wells lads, so it was just like meeting someone from your own family. They told us that Chelsea had run Cardiff from their end, and we had all missed a great day out. But, I was too tired to listen to the day's fun. I crashed out and slept all the way back home. Why had I got off that train? When we finally got back to The Roebuck that evening the General, Hickey and Match were already back, and the tale of Andy and I was ripe around the pub. After a lot of piss-taking and throwing beer at each other, things finally settled down and I eventually forgave Andy. But that was Andy, and always will be, a legend in his own bathtub!

I have had a lot of great days out with Chelsea and I remember one such occasion. It was the last game of the season, Chelsea had just been promoted from the old second division and were due to play Hull City at The Bridge. The gates to The Shed were locked an hour before the game and we were packed in like sardines. The rest of Stamford Bridge was heaving. It was a great sight to behold. We were all there the General, Match, Hickey, Mappe, Angus, Bob Desautels and Coxy. In fact, all the head hunters and nutters you could imagine were there. Chelsea had decided to do a lap of honour before the start of the game, to say thank you to the fans for a season of great support. The Shed chorus was on top form. 'Bring on the champions', was the chant, over and over again. Finally the team came out, Coxy the General and I and a few hundred more decided to run around with the team, so it was a quick leap over the barriers and on to the pitch. The police didn't seem to mind as they knew most of the faces and also knew there wasn't going to be any trouble that day. It was going to be a day for celebrations and partying.

So we ran round with the team doing our own lap of honour. When we got back to The Shed, the cries were going out "Tunbridge Wells. Tunbridge Wells, give us a wave!" How could we refuse a request like that? We all three stopped right in front of The Shed and took our bow. The Shed acknowledged it with great applause and singing, "There's only one Trevor Denton" and "General, General, give us a wave," over and over again. To Garb and me it seemed like The Shed, showing its appreciation for what the Tunbridge Wells fans had achieved, and how far we had all come from our humble beginnings. A great honour indeed!!!!

In the first half of the match, Chelsea scored and there was a pitch invasion and off we went! Just after half time, Chelsea scored a second goal. This time there was a huge invasion. Everyone wanted to congratulate the players, then 'fuck me,' thirty seconds later another goal! I think everyone in the ground was on the pitch now, the police just gave up, I think they were partying as well. I well remember a young PC saying, "You lot are all fucking troublemakers, and we all fucking hate you, but today's your day. Enjoy!" Which I thought was a nice gesture by the plod.

Chelsea got a fourth goal - a final score 4-0. The referee blew to signal the early end of the match, as I recall. We were back on the pitch again. A great day in my Chelsea career and one that is etched in my heart forever. On another occasion, Chelsea were playing at Nottingham Forest and as per usual Hickey and the General made the arrangements. It was decided not to go by Transit for this particular match but by train instead. A good excuse to get pissed and run Forest fans from their own patch. We all set off from The Roebuck, the usual crew the General, Hickey, Match, Pete J, Coxy, Angus, Bimbo and Mr Desautels, etc. Incidently, Bimbo's (Ian Cox 2) daytime job in those days was a National Hunt jockey, riding for Arthur Pitts, stable out of Epsom. He was a half decent jockey and rode about 80-100 winners in his career. When he wasn't riding horses on a Saturday he would join us for the ruck. However, if he was working we would ring him at the stables to ask him what chance his nag for that day had of winning. If he was riding an 'old donkey' he would let us know accordingly. If he was on a 'winner' we would have an 'each-way' bet. Anyone who tells me that horse racing can't be fixed is a liar. I know from firsthand experience that jockeys know if they are going to win or not. I remember two of his horses in particular, one was called Snowtown Boy and the other was Freight Forwarder. Myself and quite a few other Tunbridge Wells Chelsea lads made a few quid out of those two horses. Thanks Bimbo!!

Back to the match in question, on reaching St. Pancras, it was the usual crack, and we all 'jibbed' the train to Nottingham, even Mr. Warren! There was no chance of me getting off this rattler at the wrong place this time! We had all done the local off licence before we got on the train, so the beer and whisky was flowing freely. I had got hold of three bottles of Cinzano and a few six packs, so, by the time, we got off in Nottingham, I had managed to down about one and a half bottles of Cinzano and a few cans of beer. In fact, I was completely wrecked, but I was carried to the ground by Pete Jefferys and the General. Once we were in the City ground, I was laid out on the terraces to sober up. The match kicked off and, still feeling very unwell, I made my way to a first aid hut, which was like a large, wooden garden shed situated in one corner of the ground. I knew there would be a bed in there, so I could have a kip and sober up. I was just settling down and getting cosy, when, fuck me, Chelsea went and scored a goal. I could hear Chelsea celebrating on the terraces, which woke me up and I started swinging from the wooden sections of the first aid hut. The first aid people were trying to get me to stop, I wouldn't (so the General informs me). According to him, I was swinging like a monkey on those wooden beams. The St. John Ambulance personnel asked where I came from, and an announcement was made over the tannoy system. "Would anyone from Tunbridge Wells please come and collect your mate from the first aid hut before he wrecks it!" The next thing I knew was the door of the hut bursting open and there stood Garb and Match. "C'mon Trev," said Garb, "get down!" And with that, I was duly removed to the terraces for more fun and frolics. After the match we were escorted back to the railway station by the police on horseback, and I remember going over a bridge, which went over the River Trent. (Nottingham Forest's ground is bordered on one side by the River Trent). Anyway, as Match, Pete, Angus and I approached the bridge, we saw six Forest fans sitting on the wall, and they began to take the piss out of us.

Angus, say no more the picture speaks for itself!!

Match and Angus.

With that, I flew into one. I was still very pissed and smacked one, straight in the head. Match and I then flipped him over like a spinning top, straight into the river below, a fall of about twenty feet. The others then got brave and came at us. They all got the same treatment over the bridge and in the water. Match, the General and I looked over the wall and watched the lads swim for the bank. "That'll teach you to take the piss out of us, you Forest scum," I shouted. And then we all carried on our merry way back to the railway station. We were nearly back at the station when I felt a whack on my back and heard a voice say, "That'll teach you, you cockney bastard, don't come back to Nottingham again. You Wanker!" A copper on horseback had laid his truncheon on me, and by Christ did that hurt! I thought he had broken my back, it was a good job I was still under the influence of booze but it still fucking hurt. Angus and Match got me on the rattler ready for the trip back to London. The police were still roaming around, still smacking a few Chelsea fans here and there. Angus gave me a couple of snooker balls that he had nicked from a pub earlier with the intention of lobbing them at the Forest fans. "Feed these to the horses," he said. Just before the train pulled out of the station, I nipped off and went up to a copper on horseback. "Do you mind if I feed your horse a sugar lump?" I asked. Before he knew what I was doing, I smacked the horse in the teeth with the snooker ball. The horse reared up and the copper fell off. Now don't get me wrong, I quite like horses but not with a copper sitting on them. Anyway, I soon sobered up after that. The train was pulling out and I managed to leap on just in time. The way I saw that day was: Police 1 - Chelsea 1 - a creditable draw on the day's proceedings and not even nicked!

On the train back to London the usual card games were going on, and I was wandering down the carriages looking for the General, Match and any other Tunbridge Wells (Roebuck) lads to sit with. Unfortunately, I tripped over someone and fell on the table where a card game was going on. Money and cards went everywhere, then a voice said, "It's all right, he's a member of the head hunters from Tunbridge Wells." Unbeknown to me at the time, I had just met Danny Harkans (Eccles), Babs, and Sean, three of the hardest terrace thugs, football has ever produced. All three are living legends in the hooligan world and were known at every major league club as aggro. However, at Stamford Bridge they were treated like gods. Everyone who knew anything about soccer violence knew these greats, and I had just wrecked their card game!

Travelling to a football match was always a working class pastime and this was reflected in the clothes people wore - donkey jackets, denim, braces and the famous Doc Marten boots for giving the opposition's supporters a good kicking. This was the essential 'uniform', of, the seventies, and then in the eighties the dress code changed. The well-dressed thug wore Lacoste, Pringle and Armani. It was then easier to avoid the Old Bill and easier to get into pubs and get served. This is what Danny, Babs and Sean were wearing, when I fell across their card table on the rattler home from Nottingham. I remember Eccles saying to me, "I know you, ain't you Trevor, one of Hickey's gang?" I first thought that they were city gents coming home from a meeting, not soccer thugs. I replied to Eccles' question, "Yes, but how do you know me? And who are you?"

He said, "I know everyone at Chelsea and your reputation goes before you, now take this bottle of Scotch and go and find the rest of the Tunbridge Wells lads so we can get on with our card game. Oh yeah, tell Hickey to get in touch with me so we can sort out a new dress code for you nutters. We won't be able to get into the home end and run home supporters soon, because the police have got too much on us, so in future it's smart dress code." With that Babs, Sean and Eccles all put out their hands for me to shake. What a day and what an honour! I had just met three living legends and they knew me too.

So there was no more going into the home end, tucking our scarves in our jackets and waiting for the cry of "Chelsea boys we are here", which was the sign to run the home supporters off their own pitch and for the scrapping to begin. It was now going to be much more sophisticated dress for mingling among the home fans, but as soon as the old cry went up we were up fighting as before. So nothing new there, then! But we were looking a lot smarter and we did fool the Old Bill and got served in pubs more easily. So I suppose it was a bonus to wear the designer label gear. However, I personally preferred my Doc Martens, braces and trusty old donkey jacket or Levi jacket. Besides, you could nick bottles of booze from the off licences and donkey jackets had large pockets where you could hide them from the Old Bill and smuggle them into the grounds. An idea particularly favoured by Angus!

Still, who was I to disagree with Babs, Sean and Danny, if they stated designer gear, then designer gear it was.

On the way home after a match at Wigan, we were travelling back in a Transit driven by the General and there were twenty of us lads from Tunbridge Wells in the van. We had picked up a couple of slags along the roadside, and we were all taking turns giving them a good seeing to, on the old mattress that we used to kip on during long journeys. Hickey suddenly said to the General, "Let's stop in the next big town and go on the piss." Everyone agreed that this sounded like a good idea, even Match, who was going down on one of the slags like a wild animal, much to everyone's amusement! Suddenly, there it was - Grantham, which I think is in Lincolnshire. Anyway there seemed to be a lot of pubs, so the cry went up, "Everyone out of the van!" So off we marched to find a decent pub. Music and sounds were coming from this one particular pub and there was a disco going on, so that was the pub for us! The landlord couldn't believe his luck, twenty, thirsty football fans. His takings were going to be up for that night, or so he thought! The booze flowed and downstairs in the pub's cellar the disco was going on and the disc jockey was asking for requests. It was the time of punk music, but the DJ decided not to play any as he felt it might excite a few of the Tunbridge Wells lads, who, by this time, were well out of their heads. As I remember, it was near closing time and the DJ decided that he would risk one punk record - Big Mistake!!! He put on The Sex Pistols and everyone went mental. A monster fight erupted between us Roebuck lads and the locals in the pub. The pub and disco were virtually demolished as a result. I remember Match being thrown through the DJ's equipment. One of the local lads was carrying a knife and ended up getting stabbed with his own blade but before the Old Bill could get to the pub we were gone. A quick headcount, we were all there, then back in to the Transit to continue on our way! I bet the landlord of that pub never let any football fans in again!

Easter bank holiday and Chelsea were due to play Brighton - a nice day out by the seaside. Chelsea were planning a big day out. All the London crew and hardmen were going to be there: Babs, Danny (Eccles) and Sean, to name but a few! Coaches were being arranged and the General, Match, Andy Warren, Hickey and myself were organising a Transit from The Roebuck. We left Tunbridge Wells about 10'oclock in the morning after a few liveners in the pub. Crates of booze were loaded on to the Transit and off we set to meet up with Babs and Co. Brighton was only about one hour from where we lived, so we had plenty of time to make it there. When we got to

Brighton we made our way to The Seagull, which was the Brighton fans pub, we also met the London lads there which had been pre-arranged.

Chelsea took over the pub and there was no threat from the Brighton fans as there were only about 30 to 50 of them in there and about 300 Chelsea in and outside the pub milling about. We were all drinking heavily. It was just going to be a day for enjoying ourselves and swopping old terrace stories of previous encounters with whoever. Everytime a Chelsea fan walked through the pub door, it was like he was a long-lost relative, there was a lot of back slapping and shaking of hands. I had just bought a round of drinks when Jones, a Chelsea fan from Battersea, came into the pub. I had known Jones from a Chelsea pre-season tour to Switzerland that we had both been on years previously. We have remained Shedites and mates ever since. Before I could buy him a beer he said, "Trev, I have just gone past a pub up the road and there's a tidy firm of Brighton in there looking for trouble." I looked at the General who was sitting with Mappe, Hickey, Dave Wolvey and Match, and said, "Shall we go?" We all drank up quickly and I remember someone asking how many there were. Bobby Harbour's reply was, "Who cares! Fuck it, let's have 'em!" We marched out of The Seagull like soldiers going to war. Lead on Jones!!! The old war cry went up, "CHELSEA BOYS, WE ARE HERE, SHAG YOUR WOMEN AND DRINK YOUR BEER!"

We then bumped straight into Danny (Eccles), Babs, Sean and the London mob. Danny asked, "Aggro happening Trev?"

I replied, "Just some Brighton tossers about to get some!" Which Sean, Babs and Danny found quite amusing. "Mind if we tag along, Trev?" Blimey, what an honour!! It was like being asked by superstars to join you. We walked past Micky Dunn, Bisal, Paul Gabriel and Paul Baitup who were busy flogging T-shirts, flags and tickets for the match. Someone shouted to Sticky (Micky), "Where's Brighton?" and Sticky knew exactly where they were holed up. By this time we were 400 to 500 strong, as we had picked up a lot of other Chelsea along the way from various pubs. Sticky told us that there were about 200 Brighton in this certain pub, which confirmed what Jones had told us earlier. So we stopped about three hundred yards from the pub. Eccles decided that we would hit them from three fronts. Football hooliganism was getting more like war tactics each day. Churchill would have been proud of us. We would split into three groups.

About 150 Chelsea would come down the road from one way, then another 150 would come from another road that bordered the pub, and the rest would hit them after the main group had gone in. The element of surprise, lulling Brighton into a false sense of security. I reckon Eccles could have been a Field Marshall if he had been in the army. He was always planning great tactics against the opposition and nine times out of ten they worked. The cry went up, "Brighton, where are you?" as the first group of Chelsea walked towards the pub. There were probably about 1,000 Brighton sitting drinking outside and inside the pub, so much for Sticky's and Jones's estimate of 200! The Brighton fans thought they would run Chelsea when they realised there were only about 150 Chelsea. Chelsea went in!! Brighton retaliated, then the second wave of Chelsea ploughed in, quickly followed by the third. Chelsea were still outnumbered but Brighton must have thought that there were more Chelsea on the way, because after a lot of fighting and blood spilling, the Brighton fans scarpered like rats deserting a sinking ship. Chelsea had won the day again and it was all down to Eccles's tactical planning.

When we got back to The Roebuck that evening we gave Micky Dunn a lesson in maths - basically counting up to one thousand!!!! We were all talking about the day's events when Andy Warren walked in with Bobby Harbour, Angus and the lovely Anna. Andy looked like he had been in a road accident, "What the fuck happened to you?" I said.

Apparently, Andy, Angus Bobby and Harpo had been walking back to Brighton railway station after the match and had ben set upon by about 70 Brighton fans. Some of the fans had recognised Angus as being Chelsea, so that was that, a good kicking occurred. Seventy to four is no match in anyone's book. Andy had lost five teeth and gained a broken rib, courtesy of a steel toe-capped Doc Marten boot. Very nasty indeed! However, after getting a few whiskies inside him and some coke up his nose, he seemed a lot better. Hickey and a few others wanted to get a crew up to go back down to Brighton to sort them out on their own patch, there and then. The pickaxe handles and baseball bats were still in the Transit from the afternoon's battle. But, in the end, the beer got the better of us all and we just perched Andy up in the corner of the pub, gave him half a bottle of Scotch, and let him drift off to sleep. We all decided that he would feel a lot better in the morning and, anyway, it had been a long day for us all. Brighton would get their comeuppance another day. Chelsea don't forget!  The General and I had a talk and came up with the theory that, unfortunately, in all battles, you will always get some casualties and today Andy had been the one!

The last time I saw Eccles, Babs and Sean wearing designer clothes was when Chelsea were playing Newcastle away and, as per usual, there were about five to eight thousand Chelsea fans making the long journey north.  Now the Geordies hated Chelsea even more than they hated wearing the latest fashions.  Eccles, Babs and Sean had all the latest gear on and Eccles was also wearing gold chains and a host of gold rings on his fingers.  I remember him standing up against a fence in the galloway end at St. James Park that separated us cockneys from the Geordies and chanting, "What's it like to have no job?"  A couple of coppers saw him and threw him out of the ground.  "Wait until the local Geordies spot you, they'll fucking kill you dressed like that!"  A bunch of Newcastle fans tried but when he had been ejected he had taken about fifty allies with him, and the Geordies were very quickly despatched.  But that was the end of designer gear at away matches - thank God!  I much preferred my old donkey jacket and DM's.

A local London Derby saw Chelsea playing Charlton down at The Valley, of course, Chelsea took thousands down to The Valley. The ground was shit, it was like a giant lump of round concrete (although it has been redeveloped.  Chelsea fans were all in the covered end and soon ran out the Charlton fans.  I'm afraid Charlton thrashed Chelsea 4-0 that day.  The Chelsea fans went berserk, smashing up the ground and causing thousands of pounds worth of damage.  I recall ripping up the wooden benches that were used as seating and making bonfires of them.  They were being set alight all the way round the ground on the so-called 'terraces'.  Old plod just stood watching it happen, I couldn't believe it, the wooden boarding at the front of the main stand was ripped down.  I saw Angus and Clifford Bolton leaning out of the main stand with a 12 foot lump of 4x4 timber ripped from the advertising hoarding.  The next thing I saw was Charlie (Tunbridge Wells) trying to bash the Charlton goalkeeper on the head with it.  After all the aggro, fun and bonfires, I saw Charlie being led away by the Old Bill.  As he passed me I asked, "What did they nick you for Charlie?"  Charlie didn't answer, but the copper said, "This guy's a right hero, ain't he?  I'm going to nick him."  Apparently, the police had been pushing everyone into a corner and someone had been crushed, Charlie had shouted at the coppers, "Stop pushing, you tossers!" And so, Charlie wasn't being done for smacking the Charlton goalkeeper, he was being charged with 'using threatening words and behaviour'.

The Middlesex Arms - West-Ruislip Cup Final Day, May 14, 1994. A very bad day Man. Utd 4 Chelsea 0 (and it rained).

The General alias (Garb) in conversation with Bimbo (Ian Cox) of National-Hunt racing fame, from right to left in the picture Bimbo (woolly hat). The General, and with his back to Garb, the infamous Micky Dunn - alias Sticky Bunn - ticket tout extraordinaire and on the very far left leaning over the pub table talking to Micky, Dave Wolvey.

The Middlesex arms, West Ruislip again. Bimbo studying the horse racing form, centre of picture getting rather excited Bob Harbour and sitting next to Bobby, Scranner.

After a night in the cells, he was charged and pleaded not guilty and was subsequently bailed. I remember that there was a fucking lot of damage done at Charlton, and the next day questions were asked in The House of Commons. The front of the next night's Evening Standard had photos and stories relating to the Charlton riot. Out of thirty Chelsea fans who had been arrested, twenty- eight had pleaded guilty and were fined no more than fifty pounds, which was nothing (just a quick whip round on the next away day special)! The two who pleaded not guilty were Charlie and Mad Kevin from Tunbridge Wells. The politicians had a field day. The headlines read 'JAIL THESE THUGS', and as Charlie and Mad Kev were the only ones to plead not guilty, they thought that they would cop the lot. But when it did come to court, the copper who nicked Charlie and Mad Kev came out with the biggest load of bullshit I have ever heard in my life. He said, "My Lord, I heard the Accused shout, there's the fucking Charlton - let's beat the fucking shit out of them." Charlie and Mad Kev just couldn't believe it, they even had six witnesses in their favour. They were found not guilty, although they both ended up £400 out of pocket because they had refused costs. It's not fair justice, when you win your case but end up losing money (poor man's justice).

Violence never seemed to worry me and a good kicking was all part of the day out, but I think I was more frightened of arrest, especially when the law was changed to allow magistrates to inflict large fines on convicted fans. The Old Bill were like rival fans, some-one to pit your wits against and out-manoeuvre. Policewomen were and still are worse, as I feel they think they have something to prove to their male colleagues. Nowadays, there are thousands of police at football matches and this makes them slightly arrogant. It was better in the early days when there were only a couple of coppers. You could always have a laugh at the Old Bill, the trick was knowing when to have a laugh and how to get away with it!!!

# CHAPTER 4

## 1974-1975 TOTAL BOLLOCKS, SUNDERLAND AND THE GRAND OLD DUKE OF YORK

We were all crying in our beer in The Roebuck and had just all been through one of the worst seasons in Chelsea's history. What a load of bollocks and what a shit year. Chelsea had just been relegated to the old Second Division. I couldn't believe it and neither could a lot of the other lads. Hickey looked at Andy Warren and me, as we popped another couple of pills and said, "Don't worry lads! Just think of all the northern shit grounds we can cause havoc at next year!"

I got my head together and replied, "Yeah, Steve. I suppose it's not all bad is it?" Where's the opening game?"

"Sunderland," came the answer from Hickey. Not The Stadium of Light, as it is now, but the old Roker Park.

"That'll do nicely for an opening day riot Hickey," I said. "We'll murder the northern scum!" Plans were being made for the opening day clash, and for weeks before in The Roebuck and surrounding Chelsea watering holes, the Sunderland game was all that was talked about. Everyone knew the Northerners would be up for it as well, as they like a good punch up, but never in our wildest dreams did we expect such a reception as we eventually got when we arrived at Sunderland. Hickey, the General, Match, Angus, Andy, myself and all the other Roebuck crew arrived early at Kings Cross railway station after another heavy night of pill popping, drinking and snorting coke and the rest of the southern counties Chelsea must have had the same idea, as it was only six o'clock in the morning. There were already thousands of us milling around the station concourse and surrounding areas.

The Second Division was about to get a rude awakening. The disappointment of the poxy season we had endured last year was already fading from my mind and was being replaced with the anticipation of the thrills and excitement to come. The 'football specials' (as British Rail called them) were not what the general public would travel on, they were non-service trains supplied by good old British Rail allowing football fans to travel to away games for less money than the standard fare. I think the idea behind it was that the police could keep an eye on us fans i.e. they knew what time we left the station and what time we were expected to arrive at the other end (and, of course, we would not be mingling with the general public!) The trains were usually very old and were freezing as there were no heaters. Once you were on them drinking with your mates, nobody seemed to worry about that fact! I remember good old Micky Greenaway trying to sort out some kind of away day travel for us Chelsea and having fancy coloured tickets made up. I think he called the idea of his (CAT) or something like that, which was short for Chelsea Away Travel. It never really caught on and everyone used to jib the rattlers and do their own thing. The trains were always full and if you walked through them all you would see were tables laden with cans of lager and a lot of groups of Chelsea playing cards. There was usually someone puking up through too much booze and the toilets were overflowing. If you couldn't make the bog it was just a question of pissing or puking where you stood!! No wonder British Rail laid on the grottiest trains for our away days!!!!

The old rattler finally got us up north to Sunderland and I remember arriving at Seaburn station and opening the train window and as the train slowed down there was a tremendous cry of, "Chelsea Boys we are here!" The doors of the train all crashed open. I said to Garb and Match, "Fuck me, look at plod!" I had never seen so many police at a railway station. Obviously our reputation had preceded us. Hundreds of Chelsea were now getting off the train, some still quite pissed and being helped along the platform by their mates. As we passed the Old Bill the shouts went up, "Chelsea, united we'll never be defeated!" Over and over again. I think the Old Bill had been well briefed that day, because they just stood there and took all the abuse we could throw at them. A few Chelsea got nicked before they got out of the station but that was just for being drunk and disorderly. The rest of us were left alone, mainly I believe, because the Old Bill didn't want a riot on their hands on the opening day of the season! The Old Bill then decided to walk to the ground with us, like an armed guard. As if we needed it! But we went along with their wishes, not wanting to upset them too much at this early stage. There was plenty of time for rucking later on in the day, or so I thought. I had joined forces with Hickey and Babs and entourage. By now we were a force of about two thousand strong marching towards Roker Park like an army on Manoeuvres. All we needed was Eccles leading us from the front, anyhow, Babsy was the next best thing, and I was proud to be walking by his side. I once saw Babsy in the north bank of Highbury (Arsenal's ground) in the centre of the terracing with his crew. Arsenal knew who he was and went for him, a massive ruck followed, and the next thing I knew Arsenal were running for their lives! There was only Babsy and a few others but they had taken Arsenal's north bank by themselves. He might only have had one arm but he certainly frightened the shit out of the Arsenal and their hard men. Some people say that Babsy had the strength of three men on that day but I would say six. That day at Highbury was magic to be seen. I remember the Old Bill at Highbury jumping in to surround Babsy, when they realised what was happening on their own patch, but it was too late. Arsenal (although by this time were coming back) had been run out of the famous north bank by a few Chelsea. They would never live this down. Babsy's name was chanted for the entire match and the Old Bill made a blue safety line around him and his crew to protect them until the final whistle.

Then Babsy and co were escorted out of Highbury to safety. He had done what he set out to do and taken the North Bank almost single handedly.

Anyway, back to the plot. As we turned this particular corner of the road there was a large pub-cum-hotel, which I think was called The Railway Tavern, with hundreds of Sunderland drinking inside and outside on the pavement in their replica red and white shirts. That was it, like a red rag to a bull, as we got near the pub Babsy shouted, "Now go!" About 500 Chelsea broke ranks and charged at the Sunderland fans, glasses, bottles, chairs and bricks were being thrown at us as we surged towards the pub to get at them. The police just gave in, they were powerless to do anything even though they tried. Sunderland retreated and bolted inside the pub for safety, or so they thought, for soon the main door had been kicked in and the plate-glass windows had been smashed to pieces. Chelsea were now inside the pub climbing in anyway they could to get at the Sunderland fans. The landlord and staff were shouting, "No, no, fuck off!" But it was too late, the cues lying on the pool table were used as spears and clubs for smashing the optics behind the bar. Crash, smash, glass and bottles were everywhere. Everyone was now helping themselves to bottles of spirits, wine and fags and the few Sunderland fans that remained were quickly despatched, but to give them their due, a few of them had stood and fought, although most had disappeared out the back door to safety. The pub was now completely wrecked. There

**61**

must have been about a thousand Chelsea inside, the landlord and his staff had long since bailed out. The police sirens could now be heard. It was time to go! The whole incident must have been over in under ten minutes and by the time the Old Bill got to the pub there wasn't a Chelsea fan in sight. I'll always remember one thing that made me chuckle about the pub riot, and that was Garb turning to me and saying just as we were leaving, "Here Trev, have another bottle of Scotch for later!"

To which I replied, "Cheers Garb, what's Match up to with that pool cue now?" The juke-box was playing 'Yesterday' by the Beatles. Smash! Match put the pool cue right through the top of the juke-box, glass and bits of records were flying everywhere. "What did he do that for?" I asked Garb.

"He doesn't like The Beatles and that particular record makes him cry!" was the reply. Oh well, Que sera, Que sera.

We got hold of Match and we all ran outside the pub before the Old Bill arrived and went to find Babsy and Co. We all regrouped a couple of streets away from the wrecked pub and were quickly joined by Eccles and his mob. I was suddenly in the presence of both Babsy and Eccles. Who could have wished for more on a day out up north. As we turned another corner on our way to Roker, there they stood, Sunderland's main mob. There must have been a thousand of them waiting to give us all a good thumping. By this time, we were also about a thousand strong, and Babsy and Eccles were leading from the front giving out the orders. There were no police in sight. I expect they knew what would happen and were going to let us fight it out between us. They probably thought that us "southern softies" would get a good hiding and be 'easy meat' for their northern hard men. Wrong!!! "Walk towards them slowly, don't run!" barked Eccles. I was standing with Garb, Mappe, Match, Angus and Bob Desautels and Andy Warren and I was shitting myself! We were about ten feet behind Babsy and he looked at me, winked and said, "Don't worry, I won't let anything happen to you Tunbridge Wells lads." That was all the reassurance I needed, the adrenaline was pumping now and my heart was beating faster and faster as the two groups of warriors got closer to each other. We were now only about 100 yards away when Eccles barked again, "Everyone spread out. Walk don't run!" We all listened to Eccles' orders and did as he told us. Suddenly, a cry went up and from the side streets surrounding us and from the dirty northern alleyways came more of the Sunderland mob, flying into us from all directions, kicking and booting us. Still no sign of the plod (funny that!) But we stood and fought, I think Sunderland thought that the element of surprise of the ambush might make us run, but we are Chelsea and don't run from anyone!! I'd had that fact drummed into me at an early age on the Chelsea terraces.

The Sunderland main mob then attacked us from the front and a full blown battle began. Fists and boots were flying in all directions. Our main crew were holding up well against the first wave of the Sunderland onslaught, but, by now, a few Sunderland were getting through to where Garb, Match, Angus and I were. Garb shouted, "Use the bottle, Trev!" As three Sunderland came at me I managed to crack one of them straight on the forehead. His head split open like someone cracking a nut on Christmas day. Blood was gushing everywhere, "Lovely, nice shot!" someone shouted.

"What a waste of a good bottle of Scotch!" I thought to myself as he fell to the bloodstained roadside. Babsy, doing his own thing shouted, "Trev, watch the General's back," still clutching the bottle (which amazingly hadn't broken). I steamed into help the lads, who by now were being outnumbered by Sunderland. The bottle of whisky was above my head and I shouted something like, "You northern bastards, have some of this!" On seeing what had just happened to one of their mates, they turned and ran, probably thinking that I was a complete nutter, which of course I'm not!!! The Chelsea boots and fists were raining in on them as they tried to escape further punishment, but to no avail. They got a thoroughly good kicking. Sunderland were running for their lives, Chelsea had won the day. We gave chase and some Sunderland did stand and fight, but it was now a lost cause, the main mob hadn't regrouped and Chelsea could celebrate the first victory of the day.

Mappe, Match, Angus and I stopped by the roadside and cracked open a bottle of Scotch to celebrate and then carried on to Roker. We were now about two thousand strong and as we reached the home end of Roker Park, we chased a few more Sunderland who fled and jumped over the turnstiles. We followed suit and suddenly there were two thousand Chelsea fans in the Sunderland home end!!! The police, who we hadn't seen for ages, suddenly appeared and put a line of blue between us Chelsea and Sunderland fans. There were about a thousand plod between us, itching to use their truncheons on us. Surely we would have to wait to have another go at Sunderland outside the ground after the game, I thought to myself. The game kicked off and fuck me, Chelsea scored an early goal. Typical!! The police were busy watching the game by now and didn't notice about 50-100 Chelsea slipping past them. We were suddenly in with Sunderland who hadn't as yet realised what had happened, they still thought the Old Bill were protecting them. The cry then went up, "Chelsea here, Chelsea there, Chelsea every fucking where!' and 'you can stick your Sunderland up your arse!' The Old Bill had finally woken up to realise we had sneaked past them. Punches and kicks were rained on as many Sunderland as possible, before the police laid into us with their truncheons and threw us back with the rest of the boys. The police made an example and nicked a few faces: Finney, Brixton Charlie, Bimbo and Jock were just a few to mention. Garb and I had by now learnt when to leave it out when plods about! The Old Bill were walking down the terrace with the nicked Chelsea boys and the Sunderland fans were putting the boot in as they passed by. The police were turning a blind eye to this. I suppose they thought it was some sort of rough justice. All through the game, spasmodic fighting was breaking out around the ground, and the Old Bill kept trying to jump in and break it up, but to no avail. Chelsea lost the game 2-1, nothing has changed then! Typical, score first, then lose 2-1. "Still, at least we won the early fight," I said to Garb.

"Yeah, Trev, where've all the Sunderland gone?" he replied. They had all left early and the only people left in the home end were Chelsea fans and the Old Bill. I remember Garb asking this copper if he knew where all the Sunderland lads had gone and his answer was, "You'll find out soon enough. They're waiting outside the ground for you and we won't be there to protect you." I turned to the General (Garb) and said to him, "What a load of old wankers the northern filth are." I couldn't see or imagine the good old Fulham Road plod saying that to the away supporters at the Bridge, the away fans would get murdered. Still, I suppose the Old Bill must have thought that if they couldn't give us southerners a hiding legally, they would let their fans do it for them! Didn't they realise that we had run their main firm earlier in the day?

I looked across the car park to where the Sunderland fans were congregating and I said to Garb, "Fuck me, they've got a tidy firm down there!" There must have been about three to four thousand Sunderland waiting for us to come out of the ground. Then I heard a familiar voice rising above all others, it was Hickey and I thought what is he doing now? He was pointing at the Sunderland fans in the car park and saying, "Look at those northern wankers, they're nothing, no jobs, no hopes, living in shit holes and can't even speak the Queen's English. Let's kick the shit out of them. We're Chelsea and always will be!" Hickey loved it, the entire Chelsea crowd that remained on the terrace were listening to his every word. I think that on that day Hickey started to become a Chelsea legend, alongside Babsy and Eccles. Everyone started to cheer him and clap him, he adored it and still does. I often remind him about that day and we have a chuckle about it. "Look at the arse bandits, they're not even proper Geordies - unlike Newcastle fans," he continued. No one really worried that we had just lost the opening day's match, apart from the Chelsea players that is ! It was now time for the more serious business to begin. I was thinking to myself that we had run them once, why not again? About a thousand Chelsea finally came off the terracing and we joined forces again with Babs and Eccles. By this time we were about two thousand strong and both sets of fans squared up to each other in the Roker car park and the Old Bill (true to their word) were nowhere to be seen. I turned to Garb and said, "What the fuck happens now?"

To which he replied, "Just make sure you've got a bottle or brick in your hand Trev." I looked down and picked up a bottle (there were plenty lying around) and picked up a second to put in the pocket of my donkey jacket, just for good measure. I didn't have to wait long to discover what was going to happen. We charged the Sunderland fans and it was like lions chasing antelopes, the Sunderland fans turned and ran every which way they could. Why bother to get such a huge mob together if they weren't going to fight? I couldn't understand it. There's no doubt in any Chelsea fans' minds who were there that day that we ran Sunderland off their home terrace, ground and surrounding areas, not once, twice but three times. That day was a Chelsea victory, but not, unfortunately, on the pitch.

We all started the short walk back to Seaburn railway station thinking to ourselves, "What a load of complete wankers, the Sunderland fans are all mouth!!!" They were going to do this and that to us as we had heard through the hooligan grapevine, and all they had done was run and bottle it.

Suddenly, as we walked down this particular road, we were hit from the alleyways that run up the sides of the houses (imagine Coronation Street type houses) by a hail of missiles. Bricks, lumps of concrete, bottles and pieces of wood were raining down on us. For once us Chelsea lads had been taken completely by surprise. We had all thought that we wouldn't see anymore Sunderland until we played them at The Bridge later on in the season.    WRONG! They had regrouped and were determined to have another go at us and by this time we were in just pocket groups of about 20 to 30 each, making our way back to the station, not the 1,000 or so of before. I decided that Sunderland were still going to try and get something out of the day. Sunderland lads kept appearing out of the 'Coronation St' alleyways and attacking the small groups of Chelsea. Our particular group that day consisted of Garb, both Coxys, Bobby Harbour, Angus, Andy Warren, Match, Dartford Trevor and myself. We had to stand and fight, we couldn't run away even if we had wanted to. Fights were going on all up the street, and Chelsea were heavily outnumbered. The surprise tactics that Sunderland had employed were working. We were taking a tidy beating but we were all trying to stand on our feet and trade punches, it was like 'The Alamo' (the famous John Wayne film). There were about 30 or so lads grouped up against about 400 avenging, hostile Northerners who wanted our blood splattered across the roadsides and cobbled streets. Us few Chelsea mates were cornered in this little alleyway between two rows of terraced houses, fighting for our lives and our very existence. Bobby Harbour was being set upon by about a dozen Sunderland cunts, and he fell to the ground heaving in pain from the injuries he was receiving. I could hear him yelling in pain, as the northern boots, fists and lumps of wood were reigning in on him. The fucking northern bastards. The same was happening to Bimbo (Ian Cox) and also good old Angus. We were all trying to fight back for all our worth, but it was now looking more and more unlikely that we were going to win this particular battle. We were all getting a bloody good beating at the hands of the fucking Sunderland this time! It was going to take us all a long time to recover from this beating, that was for sure!! The injury list that day consisted of:

1. Bobby Harbour - two cracked ribs
2. Angus - broken right leg
3. Garb - broken nose and heavy bruising
4. Bimbo - fractured pelvis
5. Myself - a cracked bone in my right hand and a fractured left arm.

These had been sustained by smacking the Sunderland as hard as I could. It had been a massive battle and one of the bloodiest that I have ever encountered. A lot of punishment was handed out on both sides that day. We didn't run but just stood there, fought and took all that Sunderland could throw at us and more. Suddenly there was a tremendous roar, and the next thing I saw was Babsy and Eccles and about 200 Chelsea steaming into the Sunderland mob. Eccles, Babsy and their crew soon dispersed the Northerners and Sunderland turned and ran for about the fourth time that day. "Well done, Tunbridge Wells!" said Eccles, as he helped to pick up the injured and put his arm around us like some Guardian Angel. It made us all feel proud, but we were all in a lot of pain, I certainly was, for one!!! Amazingly enough the Old Bill finally turned up on the scene but who cared? By this time, Chelsea's reputation as being the hardest thugs in the league was still intact. The Old Bill escorted us wounded soldiers back to Seaburn station and luckily enough the special was waiting for us. We all got on board and crashed out in the carriages. Some Chelsea supporters opened a few bottles of Scotch and cans of lager and gave them to all us injured heroes to help to take away the pain. I crashed out next to Mappe and Andy Warren whilst the police were still helping the wounded back on to the train. I think they couldn't wait to get us all out of Sunderland and get the city cleaned up from the rioting and fighting that had occurred all through the day. To us Chelsea and Tunbridge Wells lads it had been quite a day out. We had smashed up their main pub at early doors and run them ragged not once, but four times. Yes, they had ambushed us on the way back to the station and we had suffered heavy casualties. They had taken some pride from that, but if it had been a boxing match, the referee would have stopped the fight early on and awarded the fight to Chelsea. We had certainly won the day, but Sunderland were still not quite finished with us yet! And as the old rattler slowly pulled out of Seaburn railway station, there was suddenly glass all over me. Smash! The windows of the carriages were crashing in all along the train. Their final effort to get at us. But as the train gathered speed, us Chelsea were finally free from Sunderland. "Fuck me, what a day out that had turned out to be!" I said to Mappe, who was nursing a dislocated knee-cap which he had acquired in the recent fighting.

"Yeah, the ugliest and most ferocious I have ever been involved in, Trev!!"

After about an hour and safely away from Sunderland, people were beginning to wake up from their well-earned sleep and were talking about the rucks and the day's events, when the door burst open and there in his suede Jacket and Levi Staypress jeans, with not a hair out of place, stood Eccles. He always looked smart even after a good fight! He was going up and down the carriages congratulating his troops as he called us, he was just like a General congratulating the troops coming back from the war. I think Eccles was really proud of us that day - the way everyone had fought for each other and the Chelsea reputation and survived to tell the tale, which we would re-live on many a night in The Roebuck and all our southern watering holes. The train was getting very cold as it was now night time, there were no windows from the carnage earlier and there were no heaters on the British Rail football specials. Well, none that ever worked that is! These were the old rolling stock that the general public would not travel on but were alright for us football supporters. Anyway, the inevitable happened, the fucking train slowed down and then stopped altogether. This was nothing unusual, us travelling fans had come to expect this of the old trains, they were always breaking down and going wrong. The next thing to happen was that the British Transport Police, who travelled with us, came into our carriage to tell us that we would be stuck there for about two hours whilst British Rail tried to get a part that was needed to get the train moving again. We very rarely saw The British Transport Police being on the same train. They were certainly never to be seen when there was any sign of trouble. Where they disappeared to and where they suddenly appeared from, I don't know and I never did really find out. When they did appear, they were just a pain in the arse. Just telling us things like: how long we would be stuck in one place, or how far we were away from a certain town. The general belief was that they spent most of the time locked up in the guard's van playing cards and getting pissed - (fucking use-less wankers). Anyhow on this particular occasion they told us we would have to wait for the fitters to arrive with the part. Fucking brilliant, stuck halfway between Sunderland and London in the mid-dle of nowhere. By now, people were beginning to stick their heads out of the holes in the carriages where the windows used to be. There in the distance were some faraway lights - it could have meant a small village or town. The next thing I knew was Babsy and Eccles were standing on the side of the railway track ordering everyone off the train. Everyone obeyed, apart from the Chelsea who were too in-jured or just too knackered to follow. "Right, we're going on a march to those lights!" shouted Eccles. So off we set. After about 15 minutes, the lights were getting brighter. Over fields we went, up and down hills and we finally arrived in a little village (the name of which eludes me). Most of us headed for the only pub in the village for liquid refreshments, whilst the others headed for the local fish and chip shop. The owner of the fish and chip shop couldn't believe his luck, as 500 football fans mingled around his shop trying to get food. The same was happening in the pub, the landlord's takings were certainly going to be up that night. Babsy and Eccles told us that we had got an hour in the village, then it was a march back across the fields to the stranded train, which hopefully by this time would have been fixed by good old British Rail fitters and would get us all back to London. We quickly gave Eccles a new nickname 'The Grand Old Duke of York' (work it out for yourself).

# CHAPTER 5

## ENGLAND

Next to Chelsea, I love England, as do most football fans. A lot of fans when they cross the Channel, feel they are representing England in a war. We have got to be better than any other country. Don't forget we won the war! I suppose that's where our ignorance comes from. I have been in many bars and hotels on the continent and heard fans asking the locals what nationality they were and afterwards saying, "Look at the Wankers, we bailed them all out of the war!" I suppose that its basically true, but I just can't be bothered with it all!! I think the craze for following England on the continent to away matches is to get a Union Jack and get your club's emblem on it so that people can see it back home on the television. But you don't seem to see many St. George's flags, which is England's flag. I expect the fans can't nick them quite so easily from hotels and other establishments back in England. The first time I travelled with England abroad was in the early seventies. The General, Micky Dunn, Angus, Hickey and myself flew from Stansted to Denmark where England were playing. Match, Clifford Bolton, Charlie (Tunbridge Wells), Dave Wolvey, Mappe and Harpo all travelled out by road and ferry. The largest groups at the England matches on the continent were always Chelsea fans, and still are. Even though Chelsea were the number 1 in the thuggery league, we never would fight any other England supporters. If you supported England, no matter what club you supported at home, you could join the England firm. Babs, Eccles and Sean didn't travel out to England away matches very often, but when they did show up, they were made most welcome. The real leader in those early England raids abroad was our own Steve Hickmott (Hickey) from Tunbridge Wells. It was a good feeling to know that all the other leaders of other clubs looked up to Hickey (from acorns grow a mighty oak.) West Ham fans would never mix with Chelsea unless there were plenty of them, and the Liverpool supporters were the same, preferring to stay in 'packs'. In fact, the Scousers used to go away with England so that they could nick anything they could lay their thieving hands on. Every club had its 'nutters'. The loonies would do really mad things which would lead to punch ups, whilst the nutters would go straight in and fight the locals and police, whatever the odds were. You had to be very careful of the two, because they could very easily get you nicked. Everybody came together to travel to England away games abroad. Twenty or thirty years ago England fans were welcomed abroad no matter what country the game was being played in. They spent their money freely and there was plenty of laughter and friendliness. But not today, an England match means entire police forces are drafted in because of the reputation of the English army of fans.

I remember going to the European Championship finals in Italy in 1980 with Angus, Match, Hickey and a few others from Tunbridge Wells. Micky Dunn and his crew were there flogging black-market tickets, flags and T-shirts as well as Bisal (rum and blackcurrant please), Paul Gabril, Bobby Harbour and Paul Baitup to name but a few. A lot of other England fans had also travelled to watch England's first game against Belgium in Turin. As soon as the fans got into Turin city centre there was aggro, and the trouble started. Fights broke out in the local bars and confrontations with the Italians began in the streets. In one bar near the ground where England were playing, Scranner, Sticky and I were minding our own business and quietly getting rat-arsed, when all of a sudden, a pavement table was hurled through the window. Glass shattered everywhere. Outside there were about 100 Italians just wanting a fight, and, of course, us English in the bar gave them one! There were about 20 of us English fans in the bar at the time, but when the fighting started, the English fans started to appear from all the other bars in the vicinity to help us. A massive battle occurred. Tables and chairs from the pavement cafes and bars were being thrown through the air at the Italian fans, and windows were being shattered. Cars by the roadside were being overturned. The local police became involved and were charging at the English fans with batons. It had turned into a first-class riot. The police then started using water cannons and tear gas to try and stop the fighting, but it just made matters worse and aggravated the English fans even more. Scranner was getting a good kicking from four Italian fans. I shouted to some West Ham lads to give us a hand, and they were quickly there helping us out, which would never have happened back in England!!! I recognised one of the West Ham fans as Alan Andrews (alias Lockjaw). Amazingly, he was a local Tunbridge Wells lad but was a West Ham fanatic. You travel all the way to Italy then bump into a Hammers fan from your hometown - amazing!!! Like I said, Scranner was getting a fierce beating, but with the West Ham fans joining in with the Chelsea and England fans, we soon saw off the Italians and gave them a few broken noses and arms and returned the kicking. The police also backed off, the place where the fighting had occurred looked like a war-zone. In the match against Belgium, England scored first, but then the Belgians equalised and the Italians in the stadium started cheering. Fighting broke out again and one English fan was stabbed by an Italian fan. I remember tearing into the Italian fans with Hickey and Scranner and getting a good kicking that day. In the end the Italian police fired tear gas into the midst of us English fans, which not only affected us but also the players.

The next match was against Italy and the feelings were very hostile and intense, the Italians were spitting all over us English fans, and the Italian police were turning a blind eye. We retaliated, of course, but were hit by the Italian police batons as they charged at us. The last game was in the city of Naples (Not the best of cities for football fans and very rough at the best of times) and the same thing happened again: tear gas, baton charges by the Italian police and brutal treatment of us English fans.

The world cup of 1990 was held in Italy. After the Heysel disaster, it was a case of kill or be killed for England fans. After the European Championships it was the World Cup qualifiers, which were to be held in Spain. There seemed no problem for England, to qualify as we were drawn against Romania, Norway, Switzerland and Hungary. The capital of Romania, Bucharest, was regarded as a right shit hole and the most boring city in the world, so the best game of the group looked like the match in Switzerland. Thousands of English fans travelled there by air and rail. Hickey, Dave Wolvery, Match, Jones and myself were just a few of the Tunbridge Wells lads that went. When we got there, we checked into our hotels and bars then it was out on the piss to get rat-arsed. We heard that a young West Ham fan had been stabbed by an Italian fan the previous day. Now everyone knows English and Italian fans hate each other, so all the English fans decided to find the Italian stronghold and give them a fucking good beating. I remember hitting two Italian fans with a chain, splitting one of their heads wide open, blood gushed everywhere, it was just a case of them or me and in this particular case I had won the day. I looked around and saw Angus laying into some more Italian fans with a half bottle of whisky, then one of the Italians pulled a knife on him. However, before you could say ice-cream, he was flat on his back in the road. A couple of Millwall fans had seen what was happening and laid the Italian out with an iron bar that they were wielding. You couldn't see that happening in England, Millwall fans joining forces with Chelsea.

There was a lot of aggro at the game as well and to make things worse, England lost 2-1. A couple of days later, England beat Hungary 3-1 and put themselves back in with a chance, which meant England had only to beat little Norway to be certain of qualifying. But, guess what? England lost!! I couldn't believe it, we wouldn't be going to Spain. All the English fans were so upset that the inevitable happened: fights broke out and bars were smashed up as the English went on the rampage. Then we heard that England had, in fact, qualified through the back door, so I could make arrangements for Spain, after all. A lot of people from Tunbridge Wells would be going to Spain but like most statements I think it was a spur of the moment thing with a lot of them. The list of definites would be Sticky, Bisal, Paul Gabril and Paul Baitup who would be flogging black-market tickets for the matches plus T-shirts and flags. Also on the list of definites were Hickey, Angus, Dave Wolvery, Andy Warren, Bimbo, Scranner, Mappe, the General, Match and myself - then there were the many maybes. Hickey, I knew, was a certainty, as he was now the number one face for England fans abroad.

The press made a bit thing about how the English fans would cause trouble but we're not stupid. We know the reputation of the Spanish police, and, who, the fuck, wants to spend their time in a Spanish jail? Bilbao was where England were to play their first three matches. It isn't the most beautiful place in the world but there were plenty of bars there! Bilbao is in the heart of Basque Separatist country, where the people do not consider themselves as Spanish. When we arrived, us English got a warm welcome, as a lot of Englishmen fought against General Franco with the Basques during the Spanish Civil war, and they had never forgotten this. The time had arrived, and we set off from The Roebuck in Tunbridge Wells for Victoria. The arrangements had been made by Sticky. He was mustard at these sort of things.

When we got to Victoria, we met up with the London Chelsea - Eccles, Danny Arkans, Babs and Sean who had a crew of about two hundred with them. The Brixton and Stockwell Chelsea were also there, led by Charlie and Finney, who were Shedites. There were also Millwall, West Ham and Arsenal in their hundreds waiting for the boat train to Paris. The train pulled into Victoria and everyone piled on to it, it was like a stampede to get a seat on the rattler - we were on!!! So it was off on the boat train to Paris, then on to Spain. The event takes place every four years, and in 1982 England was fancied to win it. We were due to play France in the first group match, and, of course, no one had tickets apart from a few fans who had managed to get some from the English FA. I think the idea of this was to stop England fans travelling, but we were all hopeful that Sticky and Bisal would come up trumps. They hadn't let us down before with tickets, when we couldn't get any. Bilbao is very near the French border so that meant a lot of French supporters would be travelling to the game as well as us English. This seemed to be a likely 'flashpoint' situation but no one was worrying about that now, as we were all just quietly getting drink down our throats. The train made its way to Dover. Once on the ferry the party really started! There were three bars on the ferry and the row of fans were ten deep trying to get served - in the end the people behind the bars gave up and everyone was helping themselves to beer, wine, food and fags. It was like a big party - Union Jacks and St. George's flags were everywhere. Everyone was singing their own terrace chants and taking the piss out of one another in a friendly way. Just before the ferry docked, everyone made sure they had nicked enough beer, spirits and fags to last the train journey into Paris. The next leg of the journey turned into one gigantic knees-up. Everyone was singing and dancing all the way. The French people on the train thought we all crazy (a few of us were!) When we got to Paris everyone piled off the train to get on the next train to take us to Hendaye, which is on the border of Spain. The next thing I knew, I saw Finney hit this Frenchman who was just standing on the station minding his own business! I said to him, "What the fuck did you do that for?"

All he said was, "Trev, I fucking hate Froggies!"

"Fair enough," I thought to myself. I looked at the General and said, "We've got to get out of here and fast, or else we're going to get nicked and won't make it to Spain." So, before Finney could smack any more Frenchmen, we grabbed hold of him and lost ourselves in the crowds. We managed to get on the train taking us to Hendaye, but not before linking up again with Angus, who, as usual, was very, very drunk. He was standing at the bar on the railway station shouting and giving this bloke at the counter a load of verbal. Angus couldn't understand why the bloke behind the bar wouldn't accept his money

- the only trouble was that Angus was trying to pay in English money and not in Francs. "Listen, you French wanker!" said Angus, "I want a beer and you've got my money!" I tried telling Angus that they didn't accept English money but he wasn't having any of it. When he was out of his head you just couldn't reason with him, but when he was sober he had a good head on him, however, this wasn't very often! Next thing I know Angus has dragged this French bloke over the counter of the bar with one hand and 'nutted him. Crack went his head! There was claret everywhere - the barman yelled something in French. Angus just leaned over the bar, grabbed what he wanted and took back his money. That would have been the end of the matter, but, unfortunately, there were a dozen Frenchmen sitting by the bar and they had seen all that had happened. I thought to myself - here we go again, and we might have got away with it but Angus turned and said to the other Frenchmen, "You want some as well Froggies?" Garb and I could see what was going to happen next, it was like slow motion. Angus kicked, over the table that the Frenchmen were sitting at. Beer and glass went everywhere and a fucking great punch-up occurred. Suddenly, from an argument between two blokes over the price of a beer it had developed into a full scale fight between about 100 Frenchmen and about the same number of English fans, who had heard the commotion and come running to help us. It was mayhem - the place got completely wrecked, the French police did get involved, but by the time they had realised what was happening the English fans had dispersed and left the scene!!

We eventually left for Spain at about midnight, at least we were on the train, but we all (Garb, Match, Andy Warren, Bobby Harbour and myself) looked terrible, we had cuts and bruises all over our bodies from the fight with the French. The next morning we crossed the border into Spain, and we felt a little better following a good night's sleep (helped by the whisky as well). Once over the border it was off the train we were on to catch the connecting train to San Sebastian. Whilst we waited at the station we all hit the bar, which I seem to remember as being very small but it had a lot of beer. Amazingly, there wasn't any trouble there, I think everyone had had enough trouble the previous day and were just too knackered. Then we heard that the Spanish in Bilbao had loads of match tickets and were ripping off the English. I hoped Sticky and Bisal had some tickets for us, or else, I could see there would be trouble ahead for us English fans. I got hold of a newspaper and on the front page it read 'the

Falklands war is over', Britain had won. I thought to myself, 'That will make the Spaniards hate us even more, because they wanted the Argies to beat us."

When we eventually got to San Sebastian, there were thousands of English supporters everywhere all going to Bilbao. Now, how were we all going to get from San Sebastian to Bilbao? Then someone had a great idea, (I think it was Andy Warren), by bus. "Bus?" I said.

"Yeah, Trev, everyone will be piling on the train and so will the Spanish police!" Andy replied. So, yes, the bus seemed like a sensible option. So about fifty of us set off to find the bus station in San Sebastian for the trip to Bilbao. The bus was due in about two hours, so again plenty of time for a drink. The first bar Angus, Match and I went into we met some lads from Cornwall who supported West Ham, and they knew Alan Andrews (Lockjaw) from Tunbridge Wells who was a West Ham fan. One of the lads was a big skinhead who had a 6" to 8" scar above his right eye and was wearing Union Jack shorts with a beer belly drooping over them. "Alright mate?" Match asked him. "What's your name?" to which the skinhead replied, "Joe, but everyone calls me Reggie."

Why Reggie? I thought to myself and after a few more lagers I found out why. Apparently he was nicknamed Reggie after Reggie Kray, one of the notorious Kray twins. The story was that a few years before, some Arsenal fans got into the Chicken Run (part of West Ham's ground) and tried to run the West Ham fans out. But Joe (or Reggie) had got hold of three of the Arsenal fans and they had not been seen at Highbury or anywhere else since that day. These three people were well-known faces and had completely vanished off the face of the earth. We didn't question Reggie anymore, but just left it there and said "See you in Bilbao mate!" to which he replied, "Yeah, let's murder the fucking Spanish cunts in Bilbao!" We then made our excuses and went to find another bar, because, I'm sure to this day, Reggie had meant what he said, and we didn't want to stay around to find out!

The bus pulled in and we all got on, it was loaded with English fans with a few locals as well. I don't think they really knew what was going on and didn't care either! The English fans were taking the piss out of the locals but it was all light-hearted. No one wanted to upset the bus driver as he was our only lead to Bilbao. There was one bloke who was ranting and raving but he wasn't English, he was French, but dressed in England colours and even had a bulldog tattoo on his arm.

He said to me, "I must drink 30 pints of lager, piss in the streets in front of people and punch some Spanish." I thought to myself, "Why on earth would a Frenchman want to support England and not his native country?" He told me that he thought the English were the toughest in the world, always had a good time and that the Government couldn't stop them and he just had to become part of the England crew! I said to him, "Fair enough Froggie, who gives a fuck what nationality you are mate as long as you fight and follow the English flag!" He seemed quite happy with that and obviously thought he had found some more English mates in me and the lads. He supplied us with booze for the entire trip to Bilbao. Good bloke Froggie!!!

We finally arrived in Bilbao and, as usual, we went to the railway station to stash our gear away in the left luggage lockers, but when we got to the station we found that there weren't any. Apparently, they had been taken out because of the threat of terrorist bombs, so the next step was to find a hotel. We found a local flea pit in the red light district of Bilbao. We checked in, dumped our gear in the rooms and went back out to the local bars looking for more English fans and to get some information about what was occurring. We found out that tickets had been sold the day before we arrived but that there were to be some more sold in the evening. That was the rumour anyway! As it was still the afternoon, that gave us a few hours to find out what the locals and the local beer were like (and also the local women). Match was an old romantic, whenever he saw an old slapper he fell in love with her, I think it went back to the Chelsea and Luton days and that infamous railway carriage!!! After a few more bars and beers we were all getting peckish, when Angus spotted some more English fans sitting outside a window. On the window there were pictures of burgers, bacon, eggs, beans and chips and also a list of prices. The fans were eating as much as they could and the windows were well steamed up. As we walked over to the place a voice said, "Alright Trev, where've you been?" It was Paul and Gary Collins, brothers from Tunbridge Wells who also supported Chelsea and who had made their own way to Bilbao by plane. After a short explanation of how their trip had been and telling them of our adventures, it was time to eat. The place was known as 'Greasy Joe's Burger Joint' and was popular with all the English fans who lived on beer and chips, which was most of us!! 'Greasy Joe's was about 100 yards from Bilbao railway station and was a must for the hungry English fans!

When you went inside the place you were hit by the heat of the cooking, there was a little counter. Behind it was a big, fat Spanish bloke who must have weighed 30 stone, cooking for all his worth!

The sweat poured off him and dripped on to everything he was cooking. He also smoked one fag after another and his fag ash would fall into the so-called food he was cooking. There was also fat and grime all over the walls. He opened up at 6.30 in the morning and was still cooking at 3.00 the next morning. You could order something and he would cook it on the spot, it would take him a couple of minutes to cook anything you wanted to eat. Once you had eaten up he would shout, "Now you pay!!" You then went up and told him what you had eaten, and he would let you know what you owed. In between serving the grub, he would also pour out beer, which was great!! Of course, everyone lied about what they had eaten but he never seemed to mind. I suppose he thought, at least he was taking a lot of money, so if the English get away with not paying for some food what the heck!!!

Dartford-Trev and Match

Match and Andy Warren having a little shut-eye.

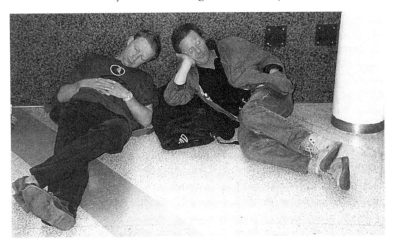

He was making a good living out of us anyway. As far as he was concerned English football fans were the greatest. It would have been easy to do a runner and leg it without paying, but I don't think many people did, as 'Greasy Joe's' was a good place to meet, drink and eat (even if in England you would have never have gone near the place.)

The night before England were due to play France, Greasy Joe locked his doors at midnight. Unheard of before! But he let about one hundred England fans sleep on his floor in amongst the fat and grease and gave them all beer, whisky and other spirits to drink as a nightcap, and to say thank you for their custom. It was that kind of place. Angus, Match, Paul and Gary Collins and myself were looking in some local bars, as we walked along the streets to the famous bullring, where, we had heard there would be tickets for the match. There were thousands of English fans milling about. We knew that somewhere would be Sticky and Bisal, flogging flags and T-shirts and, hopefully, they would have tickets. Sticky hadn't let us down before! As we continued our pub crawl, I heard a chorus of, "Chelsea boys we are here, shag your women and drink your beer!" I looked around and there sitting on a wall were Andy Warren, Mappe, Dave Wolvey, the General and Bobby Harbour. We went over to them and greeted them all like long lost relatives, which I suppose in a funny old way there were, as we were all Tunbridge Wells and Roebuck

79

lads. Sitting next to Bobby was a beautiful looking bird and Match said to Bobby, "Who's she then, Bob?"

To which Bobby replied. "Oh, I met the old sort in Paris on the way out here, she's Swedish and doesn't speak English. I've already shagged her six times, she's a great bunk up! She decided to come to Bilbao with me, I think she's in love with me, But I'm trying to get rid of her now, as I want to go mental. Do you want her Match?"

"No thanks!" Match replied, which surprised me a little bit, as both Bobby and Match were great womanisers back home. Anyway we all went into another bar. When the Swedish bird went to the ladies, we all legged it before she came back. Bobby had obviously fallen for her, as he kept telling us all what a good fuck she was. In the end, we had to tell him to shut up as he was getting on our tits a bit, so we poured a few more beers down his neck. He was soon back to the old Bobby that we had all come to love and admire.

All that was on my mind was that we still needed tickets for the match, and there was still no sign of Sticky or Bisal and no information as to where they were in Bilbao. As we continued our walk around Bilbao, we reached the top of a hill and we could hear a lot of shouting and singing coming from somewhere at the bottom of the hill. At the bottom was the famous bullring and there were about two thousand English fans, all covered in Union Jacks, St. George's flags, hats, scarves and T-shirts. Surely, Sticky and Bisal couldn't be far away? There was a mass of red, white and blue everywhere you looked. There were eight pay-windows but these were all boarded up, and had railings in front of them for people to queue in between. There were a lot of people standing in front of the windows and sitting on the railings to make sure they were first to get tickets when the windows opened. However, us lads from Tunbridge Wells just continued drinking in the bars, hoping to hear where we could get our hands on some tickets. Then a big roar went up from the thousands of English fans. The General and I thought that the ticket office must have opened, but when we looked around, we saw Bimbo, Guy, Dartford Trevor and Spud Taylor and Kim Johnson walking down the hill towards the bullring, all pissed out of their heads and chanting, "England, England!" They were swinging bottles of wine and beer above their heads These lads were all Chelsea supporters and most of them came from Tunbridge Wells, as well. Apparently, they had travelled over to Bilbao three or four days earlier and had been drunkenly walking round the streets since they had been there.

The bloke with all the hair in this picture is Guy, so called because of Guy the Gorilla from London Zoo. Guy is Ian Cox's brother and standing next to him is the author of this book Trevor Denton (Alias TD).

It was getting to be like home from home. Dartford Trev was from Dartford, as his nick-name suggests, everyone knew him. The General said to Bimbo after he had sobered up a bit, "Any tickets! Bimbo?"

"No Garb, I don't know where Sticky is. He seems to have disappeared!" replied Bimbo. Then he showed us all a Spanish newspaper. It had a picture of him and Guy on it kicking the fuck out of a French fan with the headline, 'This is an English fan - beware'. Still, it was a good picture of Bimbo and Guy, and I still have it somewhere in my scrapbook of football thuggery.

Six o'clock passed and the ticket office still hadn't opened. The England fans were beginning to get the right hump now. Then a few hundred started to bang on the wooden shutters. "Come on! Spanish cunts, open these fucking windows!" was the cry. Then to make things worse, some Spaniards appeared with loads of tickets, which they were trying to sell at rip-off prices. A few English fans paid 3000 pesetas for a 300 Peseta ticket, and a group of Arsenal fans were saying, "Don't buy off the Spanish bastards, they're ripping us

81

off." Then, all of a sudden, Guy smacked this Spanish ticket tout right in the head and blood spurted from his mouth. "Now show us your tickets, you Spanish fucker!" shouted Guy. Guy had earned his name because of his likeness to the famous Guy the gorilla at London Zoo!! He was Ian Cox's brother (Coxy) - not to be confused with the other Ian Cox (Bimbo), who was also with us in Bilbao. While the Spanish tout was wondering what happened, Paul Collins walked up to him and said, "Now how much did you want for those tickets?" The tout was still insisting on 3000 Pesetas. "Let's have a look," said Paul. The tout showed him the tickets, Paul looked at four of them closely, put them in his pocket and then calmly walked away. The tout walked after him, blood still trickling out of his mouth, and Paul turned on him and said, "Fuck off, Dago, or you'll get another slap you Spanish wanker!" The Spanish tout, seeing he was on a hiding to nothing, walked away. Paul now had four tickets, thanks to Guy. Other English fans then tried the same trick, a Newcastle fan had a go, he was fat with a big beer belly hanging over his jeans. The Spanish tout fancied his chances with this one, grabbed him round the neck and dragged him towards a crowd of Spaniards, who were gathering at the edge of the bullring. A group of Newcastle fans saw this happening, ran over and started to punch and kick the tout, making him let go and then they ran for it. Then this French bloke walked up to us trying to flog us all rosettes. He couldn't have picked a worse time to try it, by now the English fans were not at all happy to say the least! Next thing I know is Match has punched the French guy in the head making him drop all the rosettes. Andy Warren picked up the box and threw it into the air. "Now clear off you French bastard and stop ripping off the English!" There were rosettes everywhere. The local police turned up followed by the French bloke who was very angry, but by this time Match and Andy had disappeared into the local bars. There were so many English fans milling about that they would never have spotted them in a million years! They were old hands at losing themselves when the need arose. I suppose it must have been the early Chelsea training. We all knew we would catch up with Match and Andy later but the Old Bill never stood a chance. So, this French bloke started pointing out a few innocent people and the Spanish police started searching them for any stolen rosettes. By this time, there were a few thousand English fans watching events unfold and insults and accusations were flying. On one side you had the French, Italian and Spanish traders, and, on the other side, you had the pissed up England fans. Then a Spanish copper got in the middle of it all. He could speak English and it was obvious he didn't want trouble, because he knew what the English would do to Bilbao. Our reputation preceded us. He tried to calm the situation down a bit, by saying the French bloke would get nothing and should not have been there in the first place, and the Spanish traders were to return to their shops. He told us English that we should leave the bullring, because the ticket office would not be opening, as all the tickets had been sold. "What a load of bullshit!" I thought to myself as I walked back down the hill with the General, Match and Andy Warren towards the town centre to see if anyone else had any tickets. It seemed like half the people we met had tickets, and I was by now getting a bit concerned because we still didn't have any! We could always buy some from the touts, but I thought, "Fuck that" I didn't want to have to pay their inflated prices. All the lads from Tunbridge Wells met up in a little bar that we claimed for our own! Later in the night, some Millwall fans from east London came in and started talking to us. They had been in Bilbao for a week and started telling us a story, about how the night before, the local taxi drivers had had wads of tickets and were taking the piss out of the English, because they didn't have any. So, we all arranged to meet in a large bar down by the river. The rumour was that the taxi drivers were selling the tickets from a taxi-rank nearby. A couple of Arsenal fans had bought tickets for well above face value, paying 5000 Pesetas for a 300 Peseta ticket. And Taxi drivers were taking the piss out of the English fans, waving wads of tickets in their faces. A couple of hundred fans had formed a big group outside the bar. An Arsenal fan had walked across the road to where the taxi drivers were, nicked a few tickets, then ran back across the road to the other English fans singing, "You're all a load of Spanish wankers." Then Andy decided to throw an empty bottle of beer. Crash, it went straight through a taxi driver's windscreen, shattering it in pieces. I said to Andy, "Nice shot, mate!" With that, bottles were raining through the night sky and were crashing down on the taxi drivers. Some bottles were smashing the taxi drivers' windows. Rocks, stones, chairs and pavement tables were also being thrown at the cars and drivers. Andy didn't know it but he had just started a first class riot.

The taxi drivers got brave and with a few more Spanish people joining them, they came at us English fans like fucking mad animals, charging their prey! It was about 100 English to 100 Spanish. About a dozen taxi drivers came at Match, Angus, the General, Andy Warren and myself. Andy and Match knocked two of the drivers down to the pavement straight away with a pub table they had picked up. Next, I saw the General boot another one straight in the bollocks. The bloke fell to the ground as if he had just been shot. All around was blood and guts. More Spanish were turning up as well as more English fans. Then I heard a familiar voice, "Need a hand, Trev? it looks like you're a bit outnumbered." Saved from a hiding. It was Hickey, Babs, Eccles, Sean and about a hundred London Chelsea with West Ham, Millwall and Arsenal fans. We were soon knocking six bells of shit out of the dagos now. Then, a knife was flashed and one of the taxi drivers ended up being stabbed. I learned later that he had died in hospital. In the end, the police turned up. They had not been there when the fighting was going on but police always seemed to turn up at the end of trouble. Perhaps, they just didn't want to get involved and wanted to let the English and Spanish fight it out between themselves. Well that was my theory! In the end, a Scouse fan got nicked for the stabbing. I don't know what happened to him after that. I hope he isn't still in a Spanish nick, poor sod!! When it had calmed down a little, we all went back to the relatively safe haven of our little bar. It hadn't been smashed up in the fracas.

We were all in total agreement that this trouble had been the fault of the English FA. None of this would have happened if the English fans had been able to buy tickets. Fucking FA, they had a lot to answer for! A lot of other people started coming into 'our' bar and these three Manchester United fans said, "Cockneys are you, or Millwall?"

"The General and I looked at each other. "Yeah, that's right." Anyone who lives within 40 miles of London claims they are cockney. Cockneys are seen by the Northerners as having success with women and having great dress sense. Whereas, anyone north of Watford wore flat caps, ate meat and potato pies and lived in houses like those in Coronation Street. People from the likes of East Anglia were all country bumpkins, thick as two short planks and were farm workers with no money. So the General, myself and all the rest of the Tunbridge Wells crew were cockneys of a sort. "Flash gits are you then?" said one of the Manchester United fans.

"Not really," replied Mappe, "we just follow Chelsea and England."

Then another bloke said to Mappe, "Are you Millwall? Because we're looking for the 'F troop'? and their famous leader, Harry the dog, to give him a beating and to prove he's not as hard as he makes out." All of us lads from Tunbridge Wells knew Harry from Millwall and knew he was about in Bilbao somewhere as was the Intercity Firm from West Ham. Millwall's 'F troop'? and the Intercity Firm whilst on duty with England, always joined forces with us Chelsea Head-hunters. (Unlike when you were at home, where it was us against them!) But, anyway, when abroad we joined forces. This Manchester United fan thought he was really hard and kept on saying, "I want to find Harry the dog and take him out and give him a fucking good kicking!" Us lads kept telling the Mancunians that we were Chelsea not Millwall but they were having none of it. In the end, we were all getting a bit pissed off with this, so Angus said to this Manchester United fan, "If you don't fucking shut up, I'm going to smack you." The United fan kept on mouthing off saying he was going to do this and that and so the inevitable happened. Angus hit him over the head with a chair and the other two United fans on seeing this thought they would try their luck, but to no avail. Before you could say 'Old Trafford', they were both on the deck as well. Match had booted another one of them, and the General and I had taken care of the other one. We carried them outside and left them on the pavement to think about things. Funny, but we never saw them again. We didn't even get to find out their names. Still, a lot of the crews north of Watford thought they were the bee's knees, but on occasions, you just had to prove to them that the power of football thuggery lay in London and the south, not Manchester, Newcastle or the north.

The next thing I heard was that Hickey had brought a gun in Paris on his way to Bilbao, and was going to shoot any Italians he saw giving us grief. Apparently Hickey was also going to shoot the leader of West Ham's Intercity Firm as well, how true this was, I don't know!! When I was drinking with Hickey, the subject never came up, and I never mentioned it, because if Hickey had wanted to do this, he would have gone ahead and done it, no bother! But he had nothing to prove to West Ham, Millwall or Arsenal, as he was number one in the thuggery league, there was no doubt about that!!

It was midnight in Bilbao and in sixteen hours England would play France, yet there were still not many French supporters about. So the General, Match, Andy, Angus and myself decided to try and find some, so that we could wind them up, whilst the rest of the lads from the bar went to seek out the slags in the local brothels in Bilbao. The rumour was that the whores let cockneys pay half price because they liked Londoners better than the Northerners. Anyone with a Cockney accent got a bunk up for a lot less than their northern counterparts. Eventually, we stumbled upon some French supporters in a bar down by the river where the aggro had occurred with the taxi drivers. The General, who could speak a little French said to them, "Bonjour Monsieur." One of the French blokes said, "Parlez Vous francais, Monsieur?"

"Un Peu, un petit Peu," replied the General. They roared with laughter and bought us beer and wine all the rest of the night. I think we were both taking the piss out of one another, as even though the General knew a bit of French, we didn't really know what was being said, and vice-versa, but we were all too knackered for any aggro with them. So we just drank their wine, ate their food and had a laugh with them. Then we went back to our hotel for some sleep to prepare ourselves for the match the following day. Apart from Match and Angus who went to find out what the local brothels were like.

They must have been knackered because the General and I certainly were, that's for sure! I was up the next morning at about seven o'clock, I felt very ill from all the wine, beer and greasy food from the night before, but I was excited about the forthcoming match. I woke the General so that we could go in search of some tickets for the game. We went out on to the streets. England fans were eating, drinking and sitting on the pavement and in the road. Match, the General and I found a little pub-cum-cafe where they were selling snacks, French bread and seafood freshly caught that morning. We were helping ourselves, not realising that what was on the counter of the cafe was free!!! We also ordered a couple of omelettes and beers each. It was match day and as we started to eat our grub on the pavement table, van loads of riot police started to appear and kept driving up and down the road, where all us English fans were. They were looking at us very warily! We kept staring back at them and sticking our fingers up at them. I thought to myself, "Oh no, it's too early in the morning for trouble and I haven't had my breakfast yet!" Some Newcastle fans were sitting on a wall drinking Newcastle Brown ale and bottles of red wine. One of them said to the General, "Here, have a bottle of wine on us, cockneys!" Garb passed the bottle of wine to me, and I took a couple of swigs of it, "It's nice," I said to our newfound Geordie mates, although it really tasted like vinegar. I tried to put on a face as though I was enjoying it, but it was really shitty! Mind you, Geordies would drink mud if it was wet. One of the Newcastle fans said to me, "You must be a couple of Chelsea fans, because they think they can drink, but they can't really."

I said to the Geordie, "You're right there mate, You must have lead-lined stomachs to drink this muck!" They all pissed themselves with laughter, and we all started talking to each other and swapping stories. They were telling us a tale of how some Manchester United fans had been beaten up in a pub the previous night by some Chelsea fans. Garb and I didn't have the heart to tell them, that it had been us and our mates who were the Chelsea fans involved in that tale. I don't think they would have believed us, because by this time they were quite drunk. We just continued drinking their ale and having a good laugh with them, I always like meeting Geordies at England games abroad, you can always have a laugh with them.

Breakfast came and went, and at about ten o'clock, Garb and I went to look for some more mates, so we walked up the hill to greasy Joe's burger place, where we knew some Chelsea and Tunbridge wells lads would be. It was very hot and the England fans were everywhere, drinking cans and bottles of beer and wine. The riot police were still mincing about. The slightest incident would have started the trouble. We went into greasy Joe's but none of our crew were there, so we walked along a road that would take us to the San Mames stadium where the game was to take place. The bars along the way were full of English fans, and Garb and I kept popping into them grabbing a quick beer and continuing our walk. We went up to the bullring on our way hoping to find some tickets. A Spanish guy was flogging tickets but he wanted 4000 pesetas for a 300 Peseta ticket. We could have bought a couple of tickets, but we thought fuck that, another Spanish rip off merchant! We headed towards the ground. I was beginning to think that no Frenchies were turning up for the game. We went into another bar and spoke to some West Ham fans, who said they had bought some tickets that morning for 600 Pesetas. It was a fucking hot day, the hottest of the year, so we stayed in the bar drinking with the West Ham fans. The bar started filling up. Most people that were coming in seemed to have tickets either having bought them at the inflated prices or having nicked them. Then, some French supporters came into the bar, flashed a load of Pesetas and cried out, "Beer for everyone!!" This French guy was buying beers and spirits for everyone, one of the West Ham lads said, "Be careful, he's probably queer." But all he wanted to do was promote harmony between the French and English fans, he kept saying,

"May the best team win."

By now it was about 12'oclock and the French supporters were turning up in their thousands. Most of the English fans and nutters were drinking and getting quietly pissed in the little local bars that were in a square situated just behind the stadium, where the game was to be played. The bars were all packed to the rafters. It was great and I loved it. I was in my element, knocking back the lager and cheap Spanish beer that was on offer and popping the odd pill, what could be better, I ask you, than to be getting stoned with your mates, talking bollocks and watching football, pure bliss!! The General (Garb) and myself had found this particular bar and in it were all the Tunbridge Wells crew: Hickey, Dave Wolvey, Angus, Match, Andy Warren, Bobby Harbour, Mappe, Paul and Gary Collins, in fact, half of Tunbridge Wells!! Also, there were Eccles, Sean and all the London Chelsea. Hickey said to me, "Where've you been, Trev? We thought you and Garb had been nicked."

"Not yet," I replied, "Buy me a beer, Hickey!" The riot police by this time were everywhere. Opposite our bar on the other side of the road was another bar called The Winston Churchill, this was packed with northern supporters, Leeds, Manchester United and Newcastle fans. We stood outside the bar asking about tickets. Everyone seemed to have one but none to sell. I still felt confident that I would get one though. Bus after bus came along the road packed with French fans and they were all waving at us, most of them were wearing their national colours. Suddenly, I heard a shout, "Trev!" It was Ferret (Graham Haines) another Chelsea nutter from back home. Ferret was so called because of his small size, and he could squeeze into any ground, but a right hard nut and good fighter. He was walking up the road with his mate Steve (Southborough) Bridges with whom he mostly went to Chelsea and England matches. They both came from the same area of Kent, where most of us other Chelsea came from. We greeted each other like long lost brothers, then Ferret said that he was staying in the same road as the General and me. Then he said he had bought a couple of tickets for 1000 Pesetas, and that pissed me off a little bit as I still didn't have one! I was still confident I would get one but where was Sticky?? There were only two hours to go to the match now. I spotted another Spaniard who had tickets, and I asked him, "Tickets?"

"Si Senor," he replied. I asked him what he had got, and he pulled out a couple of tickets with a face value of 1000 Pesetas each, "Very good seats," he said.

"How much?" I asked.

"900 Pesetas," he replied.

"No, too much!" I replied and pulled out my money and gave him 400 Pesetas, he looked at me and said,

"No, English, 900 Pesetas." He had already passed me the tickets, and I had put them in my pocket. He gave me my 400 Pesetas back, so I now had two tickets and all my money back. However, I felt a bit sorry for the tout, so I said to him, "Now look here you onion basher. I'm giving you a good deal, either take what I'm giving you, or you won't get anything." The General knew exactly what I was planning because I still had the tickets and the money, a runner was on the cards. There were still thousands of English and French about in the roads, so to get lost in the crowds would be easy. In a flash Garb said to me, "Leg it, Trev!" So, before the Spanish tout could say 'omelette', Garb and I had done a disappearing trick into the crowd and had gained two tickets for free!! As it happens they were really good seats, worth about twelve pounds each. The General and I had a couple of beers in another bar and were really chuffed with ourselves for getting one over on the Spaniard. Then, fuck me, just as we were leaving for the terraces, I heard this familiar voice, "Shirts, flags, get your England T-shirts here!!" It was Sticky with Bisal, Paul Baitup and Paul Gabril flogging their wares. I went up to Sticky and said, "I've been looking for you everywhere, where the fuck have you been?"

"Trev," he said, "we got nicked two days ago and have only been in Bilbao for a day." Apparently, Sticky got his collar felt (nicked) for not having a local licence to sell his gear. "Got any tickets, Mick?" I asked. To which he replied, "How many do you want, Trev?" He then produced about fifty tickets.

"None!" I said, "I've ripped off a Spanish tout!" He laughed and told us that he would have let us have a couple of tickets for five hundred Pesetas. I told him that if it had been the day before, I would have bitten his hand off but thanked him anyway!!

I directed Sticky and Bisal to the bar where the other Chelsea lads were drinking because if they didn't have any tickets, Sticky could unload them in there, if not they could always flog a T-shirt or two!!

The heat was now so hot it was burning your feet just walking along the road, but it was now time to go into the ground. Everybody was buying bottles of water to drink, and the local shops were running out of it. I remember a couple of English fans passing out on the terraces because of the heat. How anyone could play football in weather like that I just don't know!! There seemed a lot more French supporters in the ground than there were English fans, but everywhere you looked there were the flags of the English and French supporters waving in the calm breeze. The match kicked off and after about a minute, it happened, England scored! Everyone went mental, I was standing with Match, Andy Warren, the General and Bobby Harbour at the time, and I grabbed hold of Match to celebrate in delight. In fact, I grabbed him so hard, he collapsed in pain. At first, I thought I had broken his ribs, but I haden't, but he was in pain for a couple of days afterwards. He soon forgave me though!! I looked around and saw Andy Warren kissing this big, fat Geordie supporter, ah!! Everywhere you looked the English fans were going crazy. There were a few little skirmishes going on between some French and English supporters, but it wasn't anything too serious and quickly settled down. In fact, the mood inside the ground was quite relaxed, as everyone was happy!! Then late in the first half France equalised, the french supporters near us started to celebrate. This was like a red rag to a bull to some Manchester United fans who decided a fight was in order and went steaming into the Frenchies. A big fight occured between the two and I'm afraid to say that on this occasion the English came of worse, perhaps it was because us cockneys never joined in - if it had been anyone, but Manchester United fans, I think we may have helped. However, they always seemed to be so smug and arrogant when abroad and kept themselves much to their own little groups, never really joining in with the rest of the English fans. Que sera, sera, I suppose!! Anyhow, there were a few arrests as the Spanish baton-charging police waded into the crowd, beating people around the head and arms and, before they had to resort to tear gas, the situation was soon under control. The Spanish nicks would be heaving tonight, I thought to myself.

The second half started, and England were playing much better, I think they must have got a bollocking at half time. England scored twice more and the final score was France 1, England 3. At the end of the game, the French supporters near us were congratulating us on a fine victory, they all seemed to want to shake our hands and kept on saying, "tres bon" to us and that Bryan Robson was "magnifique". They hadn't understood what all the fighting had been about and we just told them, "Oh, they're from Manchester," and left it at that. I don't really think they understood what we were saying, but we did and that was all that really mattered.

After the game had finished, we all left the ground. We were dancing and singing as we walked down the street. The Spanish riot police were everywhere and didn't know what to make of us English fans. The General, Bobby Harbour, Match, Andy Warren and I met up with the London Chelsea, Babs, Eccles, Scan and co in a large cafe-cum-bar that was in the centre of Bilbao, it was packed to the rafters with English fans. Sticky, Bisal and their crew were there trying to flog T-shirts and flags, and Hickey and his mob of head hunters was also there as well. In fact, I think if the Old Bill had thrown a net over that bar on that particular night, they would have scooped up every serious soccer hooligan in England. After a few hours of getting pissed, celebrating and losing a lot of money playing cards with Sean (will I ever learn?) it was time to move on. Match said to me, "Come on Trev, let's go down to the red light district and find some old slappers and give them a good going over and fuck them silly to celebrate England's great win!" I looked at the General and asked him if he was up for it.

"Yeah, Trev let's go!!" he replied. So off we marched, "Anyone else coming?" shouted the General and with that, Angus, Andy, Bobby, Mappe and a few others got up from their pissed up state to come with us!!! I'll always remember there were quite a few pretty ones in the windows of the red light district of Bilbao plying their trade. Well, they all look nice and pretty after you've had a couple of bottles of Cinzano, San Miguel beer and cheap Spanish wine down your throat, don't they? We all paid our Pesetas and had our wicked way with the old sorts. But Andy, who was out of his head by this stage on beer, pills and Coke (up his nose), picked this fucking fat old bird who must have weighed about 30 to 35 stone in weight, was as ugly as an old pig and must have been about 70-80 years old!! In fact, she could have been Greasy Joe's wife of the burger bar fame. She smelt of onions and grease, and I shouldn't think she had seen a bar of soap or water in years. Still, Andy seemed happy with her, she had gigantic tits that lay halfway down her waist like double footballs and talk about spare tyres, I think she had a whole car wrapped around her, what a dog!!! Andy itched for weeks after that and I'm not surprised, but he seemed extremely happy with himself after his experience. But that's Mr Warren!!

After we all had enough of the red light district, it was time to hit a few more bars, but by the time we had all grouped together again it was about three o'clock in the morning. We all decided to get out of Bilbao for a few days, before England's next match, which was due to be played a couple of days later back in Bilbao. So, we all went back to San Sebastian the next morning, which is a very pretty little Spanish town, in fact, most of the English fans were moving out of Bilbao by now, and were also going to come back when the next match was on!!! We caught the bus to San Sebastian. I don't think anyone paid their fare on the bus, but the driver was quite happy with that, as he didn't get his bus smashed up by drunken English fans. Sticky and Bisal were also on the bus and gave the driver some shirts and flags for his family, so he was happy and didn't worry us and let us have a free trip all the way!!

When we arrived in San Sebastian it was very difficult to find accommodation to stay in, all the half decent hotels seemed to be already booked up. The General, Andy and I went into this one particular hotel, which was a bit of a flea pit and asked the porter behind the counter if he had any rooms left. He told us that the last football fans who had stayed there had been very rude to his other residents, and had been sick all over the hotel, and urinated in the rooms and lifts. We told him that we were not like that, and after a lot of discussion, he agreed to let us have a room. The room was quite large and was fairly nice as it happens!! It was also on the ground floor, which was a plus as it meant being able to open the window at night and let other fans have a kip on the floor, without the owner knowing. And it was also handy for sneaking the local women back for a quick shag. After we had a sleep, it was out on the town to see what San Sebastian had to offer. San Sebastian is a typical Spanish town. The English supporters were drinking mainly at a couple of places in the centre. I remember one was called Club Hollywood and the other was called The Twickenham Bar. I think it was so-called because the owner liked rugby. Anyhow, most of the Tunbridge Wells crew and the London cockneys were drinking in The Twickenham, so it was there that the General, Andy and I settled. The General and I quickly learnt a few phrases of the Basque language because anyone who ordered a drink in the Basque Language got a larger measure than if they ordered it in either Spanish or English. The owner explained to us that the Basques had a different flag and a different language from the rest of Spain, and he preferred people to speak in Basque. We all drank heavily and swapped tales of all our exploits in Bilbao until the small hours of the morning. At about three in the morning, the General and I went back to our hotel, and as we both staggered along the road, we bumped into Hickey, who was staying just along the road from us. He said to us, "I've arranged a football match in the morning on the beach between us cockneys and the Northerners, are you and the General going to play?"

"Yeah," I said to Hickey, "see you down on the beach in the morning, mate!"

"Don't be late, kick off will be at ten o'clock!" he said.

"OK," I replied. The General and I, however, didn't wake up until 10.30 the next morning and, by the time we got to the beach it was eleven o'clock. Hickey called out to me and the General, "Hurry up lads, you're late and we're already three goals down to the Northerners." So, Garb and I joined in and, by the end of the match, we had managed to turn the game around in favour of us cockneys. I think the final score was something like ten-six, anyway we won, and Hickey was happy about that. I even got my head in the way of one cross and scored a goal, which was a rare occurrence for me, because I've never been that good at football. After the game, we all sat about on the beach, just drinking, swimming in the sea, having a laugh with the Northerners and listening to music from Hickey's giant stereo. Then, Hickey started to tell us about how the night before some Scousers had stolen some money from a Spanish girl in the Club Hollywood, and had created a lot of bad blood between the English and the Spanish. Now, Hickey is no angel by any stretch of the imagination, but thieving by Scousers was right against his religion, so a punch up was on the cards. So, off we all marched that evening to find the scousers in the Club Hollywood. There were two burly Spanish bouncers on the door stopping people who looked like they might start trouble from going in. "Cockneys?" asked one of the bouncers.

"Yeah, so what?" replied Hickey.

"You're not welcome in here," said the other bouncer.

"Then tell the thieving Scousers to come out here then!" Hickey said to them.

"Fuck off,' said one of the bouncers in his broken English. It was the worst thing he could have said to Hickey - Smack - Hickey landed a good punch straight on the bouncer's nose. Blood spurted everywhere and, as he went down on the floor, the boots of the other lads started to rain in on him. The other bouncer got brave, but before he could try to defend himself, Match had picked up a chair and hit him over the head with it.  Again, the blood was gushing out of a head wound and he also got a good kicking.  Hickey said, "Well, that's the bouncers sorted out Trev, where's the fucking Scousers?"  As we marched into the Club Hollywood a lot of the Spanish women and men who were drinking in there looked at us.  Hickey told them, "Don't worry, you're safe, it's that shit in the corner we're after!"  In the corner of the club were about thirty Scousers.  One of them must have been their leader and he said to Hickey, "Do you want some, you cockney bastards?"  With that all hell let loose.  The main Scouser with all the mouth was soon on the floor pleading for mercy as Angus and the General set about him, and, when he wasn't looking Andy put a bottle across his head.  Well, it was us or them.  The rest of the Scousers got a good battering, and the place got completely smashed up.  We left our calling card - 'you have been visited by the Tunbridge Wells Head-hunters' - the General dragged the so-called leader of the Scousers up by his hair and said to him, "I'm sure you won't be nicking anything again, will you?"  And before he could answer, the scouser got a final couple of boots in the bollocks for good measure.  Funny thing was we never saw those Scousers again after that, but we invited all the Spanish in the club down to our bar to say sorry for smashing up their place.  A few of us had our wicked way with the senoritas that night, I think they liked cockneys, yeah, there was a lot of shagging on the beach on that particular evening.

England were due to meet Czechoslovakia in the next match, so it was back to Bilbao to get tickets for the game.  All the Tunbridge Wells lads travelled back to Bilbao together.  Andy and Bobby found this great pub in the old part of town, where the local people ate.  I think the owner liked the English fans because he kept supplying us all with free wine and free beer.  The grub was really good too, unlike Greasy Joe's burger place just up the road.  One night, the General, Match, Angus, Andy and I were enjoying a meal when these Northerners who were sitting by the main door decided to do a runner.  That was the last straw, the owner turned against all the English fans after that and we never got any more freebies, so it was back to Greasy Joe's burger place!!  The owner had associated us all with the Northerners that didn't pay for the food and so we were all barred.

The day of the match arrived, and everybody was drinking in the bars as usual, some England fans had gone to Madrid to try and buy tickets for the final, which they hoped England would get to, but the General and I were not sure that they would make it to the finals.  We found Sticky and Bisal and they had wads of tickets for the match, so the General and I paid Sticky 300 Pesetas for each ticket, which was about face value - as Sticky's a Tunbridge Wells lad and one of us, he didn't screw us up, he wouldn't dare!!! A few Northerners saw Sticky flogging the tickets and came over to where we were. "How much for a ticket, mate?" this Newcastle fan asked Sticky. On seeing they weren't Cockneys or Chelsea, Sticky replied, "1500 Pesetas to you mate."

The Geordie replied, "Right, give me four," and he handed over 6000 Pesetas and Sticky gave him his four tickets. The Newcastle fans went away quite happy paying 6000 Pesetas for four tickets with a face value of 1000 Pesetas!!! A quick profit of 5000 Pesetas (about £20 Sterling) for a minute's work - nice work if you can get it, I thought to myself. As the Newcastle fans walked off down the road, Paul Gabril (one of Sticky's shirt sellers) shouted, "You don't want to buy any shirts or flags as well, do you?" We all laughed, Newcastle fans are always good for a laugh but have no idea of money. Bisal called to them, "If any of your mates need tickets, tell them where we are." I think Sticky and Bisal could see a good little earner appearing!!

After we had got our tickets the General and I said to Sticky and his crew, "See you later for a drink" and we wandered off to find the rest of the Chelsea and Tunbridge Wells lads. As we walked down the road the General spotted Andy Warren, Mappe, Match and Angus sitting in this little bar, so we popped in to join them. The drinks flowed and soon it was the evening, and most of the London Chelsea were in our bar with the rest of the Tunbridge Wells lads. A sing-song and knees-up started, everyone was having a good time. Sean, Babs and Eccles had a card school going in one corner of the bar and were skinting everyone that sat down with them. I chuckled to myself as I stood there and watched, because I had learned the hard way many years before. You don't play cards with Sean, he was a master at it. In this one particular hand, Babs and Eccles had dropped out and it was just Sean and this Arsenal fan left in the game. The Arsenal fan thought he was a bit of a card sharp, and all his mates were standing around watching him put his money on the table. There must have been about £300 Sterling on the table and the Arsenal fan said to Sean, "I'll see you then."

Sean replied, "That'll cost you £50." The Arsenal fan slapped another £50 on the table and asked Sean what he had got. Sean turned his cards over one by one, his first card was a King, then he turned over another King. The Arsenal fan went to grab the money and said to Sean, "A pair, is that all you can manage? I've got eight, nine, ten!"

"Not so fast!" said Eccles to the Arsenal fan and Sean flicked up his third card, it was another King, a priole of Kings!!! The Arsenal fan couldn't believe it, Sean had cleaned him out. I think that they would have caused trouble, but when they realised who Babs, Eccles and Sean were, and that Hickey and the rest of us Tunbridge Wells lads were still in the bar, they thought better of it and just left very quietly. Eccles just said to them in his commanding, authoritative voice, "Fancy a game of cards any other time lads we're always here if you want to lose some more money!" and laughed his head off to the fact that Sean had just taken the gooner (Arsenal) fan for a right mug. Sean gave Babsy and Eccles twenty quid each and settled down on his chair with a bottle of Bells beside him, which he was gently sipping while waiting for the next mugs to walk through the door. Three card brag was always Sean's game, he was mustard (very-good) at it. He was also shit hot at poker, as Italian Danny of Danny's Cafe fame (Tunbridge Wells) could tell you, to his loss. I once saw Sean take Danny for £550 in just one hand of poker, and Danny thought that he could play a mean game of poker! Danny was crying in his pasta for weeks after that experience, but he still went back for more. Why, I shall never understand. If, I so much as lose £15-£20 playing cards I am pissed off! But Sean and Danny were and still are major league players when it comes to card schools, (well what I call major league players) perhaps not quite in the very, very big $ league as yet but well on the way to being up there, (Scary!!) Sean saw me watching him clean out the Arsenal fan and turned to me and said, "Do you fancy a game, Trev?"

To which I replied, "Sean, you have got as much chance of me sitting down and playing cards with you, as me being the next striker for Chelsea, or me being the next man to walk on the moon!! You must be joking!" To which Sean and Babs and Eccles found highly amusing and laughed amongst themselves. "Here Trev," Eccles said to me, "have a tenner and buy yourself a bottle of wine or a couple of beers, we love you Tunbridge Wells lads you are always up for the crack!"

Next thing I knew, was that about a dozen Scousers walked into the bar (you can spot a Scouser a mile away - they have a certain look about them). Anyway, Hickey saw them walk into the bar and said to the General, "Here we go again Garb, remember Club Hollywood the other night?"

Hickey went up to one of the Scousers and said to him, "Out, what do you lot want in here?"

The Scouser replied, "We're skint. Give us some money and have a whip round for us." Before the place erupted into a fight, Babs and Eccles, who had seen what was about to happen, got up from their card game, went over to Hickey and said to the Scousers, "We don't want your sort in this bar. You're nothing but thieves and liars, always gibbing in places and doing runners. Now fuck off!" The Liverpool supporters had a quick look round the bar and realising they were on a hiding to nothing just disappeared into the Spanish night. We then settled back down again, drinking and having a good time till the early hours of the morning. We knew there wouldn't be any trouble at the match with Czechoslovakia, as their fans wouldn't be able to travel, because they were unable to get travel visas very easily. So, it was just going to be us England fans at the match.

The Match started and England were playing well. Most of us Tunbridge Wells and London Chelsea were gathered behind a goal. England won the match 2-Nil. After the match everybody started dancing on the terraces. All the England fans made a giant 'Conga' and were going up and down the terraces. The Spanish police didn't know what to make of us English fans - all the English fans were now spilling out on to the street in one giant conga. The riot police followed us thinking that at any time we were going to cause trouble. We all thought that after this win, England would win the World Cup. Everyone hit the bars to celebrate (as per usual) that evening.

In the morning Hickey arranged another game of football on the beach between the Northerners and us cockneys and a closely fought battle saw us cockneys triumph again. After the footie match, we all went back to the The Twickenham bar (which us Tunbridge Wells Chelsea had claimed for our own). The General, Mappe, Match, Angus and I were sitting quietly getting pissed, when we heard that the riot police were raiding bars and beating up any English fans they could find. Why? I don't know. Next thing I knew were the doors of the Twickenham bar bursting open, and in charged about half a dozen riot police armed with machine guns. They started hitting any-one they could get close to. The General, Mappe and myself got smacked around the head, arms and legs and it fucking well hurt, I can tell you!! The riot police seemed to be enjoying what they were

97

doing, they grabbed a couple of West Ham supporters who were with us at the time and took them away. I still don't know, to this day, the reason why they acted this way. After they had left the bar, the owner (who we had got to know quite well) served us free beer and spirits for the rest of the night, and this helped to ease the pain of the beating enormously. The next day, I had bumps like eggs on my body and cuts all over, as did a lot of the other lads. Match spotted the West Ham lads drinking in a nearby bar and went over to them to see what had happened to them. Apparently, the riot police had taken them to the police station and had beaten them up in the cells. I called them over to where we were sitting and bought them a couple of large Scotches each. I know they were West Ham fans, but it was the least I could do, I felt a little bit sorry for them, thinking to myself, it could easily have been any of us Tunbridge Wells lads who had spent the night in the Spanish nick!!

The next match England were to play was against Kuwait. England won this match 1-Nil. After this win, we all thought winning the World Cup was a certainty, but as so often happens in football, we failed at the last hurdle, losing to West Germany and Spain. So, in football terms, that was that!!! We were all a bit pissed off by now, and I remember sitting in a bar with the rest of the Chelsea lads, drowning our sorrows. I was talking to Andy Warren, when he started to scratch, "Are you alright, mate?" I asked him.

"Trev, I think I might have caught a 'dose' from those old slags in the red light district in Bilbao," he replied.

He asked me if I was feeling OK. To which I replied, "Yeah, I don't think I've got the pox." Then we heard that there was a hospital in Bilbao that gave free check-ups for English soccer fans. I think a lot of the lads, who had gone to the red light district after the match with the French, had ended up with a dose. Perhaps, I was just lucky. I found it quite funny though, as it meant that Andy and the rest of the lads who had caught a packet, wouldn't be able to drink alcohol anymore, due to the penicillin treatment. I just hoped poor Angus hadn't caught it, because he would be on tomato or orange juice for the rest of the trip, and to him that would have been worst than getting the pox!!

After the World Cup fiasco, England got a new manager, out went Ron Greenwood and in came Bobby Robson. His first match in charge was in Copenhagen. The match didn't matter much to us fans. I think the score was 2-0. Bobby Harbour, Match, Andy Warren and I went, as usual. Of course the usual trouble occurred, but I think the Danish fans were looking for trouble from the word go. They certainly got trouble from us English fans. I think most of us hooligans, that made the trip to Copenhagen, knew we wouldn't get nicked, or have to face prison. All the Danish authorities would do, was to deport any troublemakers out of their country. So, it was the green light for us all to cause as much damage and mayhem as we could!!

After Copenhagen it was on to Budapest, this was the best ruck and the most amount of trouble that any English hooligan will ever have caused abroad. The football fans behind the 'Iron Curtain' were certainly not far behind their English counterparts for fighting and trouble. As far as I'm concerned, they're a close second to us for hardness, they just don't bottle anything. Fereneveros were the local team in Budapest. All of us English fans travelled to the NEP stadium on the rattler. When we pulled into the railway station, the Hungarians were waiting for us in their thousands. As the train arrived, bricks, stones and bottles rained down on us and, the next thing I knew, was there was a massive punch up in the station.

When the riot police finally turned up at the railway station after about two hours of fighting, all they did was to help their own Hungarian fans and turn on us English fans with baton charges and water cannons, which made the situation much more hostile. A lot of English fans returned home that day with broken arms and other battle scars, without ever having left the station. After a while the riot police managed to get a grip on the situation by using the water cannons. It was still the best fight ever had by the English on the continent. Ask any hooligan worth their salt and they will tell you.

The best part of our trip to Hungary, apart from the fight, was ripping off the Football Association and the then Secretary, Ted Croker. The FA never like England fans travelling and thought they were a law unto themselves. They really hated us Chelsea fans the most. I think the reason for this was because we always tried to mince our way into hotels where the English players and team officials were staying. We would drink in the bars of the hotels and try to get tickets for the matches from the players. Sometimes, we would get lucky and get some complimentary tickets, especially from players who were not going to figure in the match. I remember on one occasion, when Hickey, Match, Andy and myself were in a hotel bar and the Football Association people were staying there as well. The FA had set up a table in the foyer. The idea was, that people who were on a special list, could walk up to the table, state their name and claim their tickets for the match. So, I said to Match, "Go up and see if they have got any spare tickets, Match!" Match went up to the table where the FA were sitting, before he could speak, the bloke behind the desk said, "We haven't got any spare tickets - especially not for Chelsea fans." But Match was not prepared to be fobbed off by an FA official. He clocked (saw) a name on the top of the list and said to me, "Trev, go up and say your name is B. Murray, I saw his name on the list." So, off I went up to the table and said to the gentleman behind it, "Good day, I'm Mr. B Murray, and I'm here to get my tickets." I was asked to sign a form and was handed a pair of tickets. I thanked him and went back to where we were all sitting, "Great idea, Match!" I said. I had also noticed another name on the list S. Thomson, so I told Andy to go up and do the same thing, which he did. He also came back with another pair of tickets, he gave one to Hickey and kept the other for himself. It was a great trick. Some other Chelsea sitting nearby also tried the same with success. The drinks flowed and all of us Chelsea fans were as happy as pigs in shit. We had completely fooled the Old FA. Then that old rascal, Ted Croker, the secretary of the Football Association came up to the table where we were sitting and said, "No luck with tickets then, lads?" We all got our tickets out and flashed them in his face. He couldn't believe it. It was the biggest piss take of all time and the Football Association were left with egg on their faces!!

After the match in Hungary, the fans of Fereneveros wanted another fight with us, but the local riot police had a tight grip on the situation. However, Hickey, who was by now the established leader of the English fans, had different ideas. He had a map of the local streets and he had decided that we should come up from behind and hit the Fereneveros fans. This was a bloody good idea! A gigantic punch-up happened.

The newspapers started to call Hickey 'the General'. His name General Hickey (not to be confused with Garb - the General) was made many years earlier when he used to organise away travel, terrace tactics and fights for us Tunbridge Wells Chelsea from HQ: The Roebuck public house, Camden Road, Tunbridge Wells.

The finals of the European Championship were coming up, and England were due to play Luxembourg away from Wembley. The Luxembourg officials didn't like the idea of having all of us hooligans in their small country, but all us Tunbridge Wells and London Chelsea and the other groups of England supporters were going. It looked like the ideal country for a big punch-up. By this time, a lot of Roebuck lads had discovered another pub in Tunbridge Wells The Kelsey Arms, which was about half a mile away from The Roebuck. The Roebuck was beginning to get a lot of visits from Tunbridge Wells plod and a lot of hangers-on were drifting in on our scene. Hickey, Match, Andy, the General and myself had a rethink of the situation and decided that another pub was called for. The Kelsey was a very large pub on the main road into Tunbridge Wells and all us Chelsea lads got to know the landlord and landlady, Mick and Debbie Tainter, very well. Mick was an Irishman, who supported Arsenal, but when all us Chelsea lads were in his pub, he was a Chelsea man. I think he liked Chelsea as much as he liked Arsenal after hearing all of our stories! The Kelsey's claim to fame (apart from us Chelsea lads!) was the pool team, which used to win the local league every year, thanks to JF (John Francis) and one of the other players in the team, Sean O'Callaghan. Now, I had many a good drink and mental session with Sean and he was a really good bloke for a laugh and a drinking session. One morning, I was reading the Daily Mirror about the bombing at the Grand Hotel in Brighton. The bomb had blasted the hotel in half when the Conservative Party were staying there for their annual conference. Maggie Thatcher was the Prime Minister at that time and she and most of the other Government officials were in the hotel at the time of the blast. I thought to myself that the IRA have struck a blow again for what they believe to be justice, and then I went on to read the football on the back pages and thought no more about it. A couple of weeks went by, and I was reading how the anti-terrorist police were looking for 'The Jackal', who they believed was responsible for the bombings in England at that time. 'The Jackal' was the most wanted terrorist, in mainland Britain at the time all the police forces in the country were looking for him. The next thing I knew, there was a picture of Sean in the Daily Mirror. I heard that Sean had walked into Tunbridge Wells police station and said to the desk sergeant, "I think you have been looking for me."

The desk sergeant said to him, "Who are you then son?" to which Sean replied, "I am Sean O'Callaghan, 'The Jackal', responsible for the terrorist bombings in England." The desk sergeant couldn't believe his luck - standing in front of him was the most wanted man in England, and he had simply walked in and given himself up. Sean was put in a cell and Scotland Yard were summoned. Sure enough, Sean was 'The Jackal'. He was extradited to Ireland and imprisoned in H-block of the Maze prison in Northern Ireland.

I just couldn't believe it, Sean, the bloke I had played pool with for a couple of years, was the most wanted IRA terrorist of all time. From that day on, every time I was in The Kelsey, I saw Mick (Murphy), the landlord in a completely different light. Above the pub were two function rooms, where parties and wedding receptions were held, and it was also where Sean had lived, so I put two and two together, Sean - Irish and Mick - Irish!!! I was never quite sure about Mick after that occasion, but he was our mate and that's all that matters. That was the last I heard of Sean and, as far as I know, he's still in prison. It was amazing really, no police force or Scotland Yard could find him. If they had nipped into The Kelsey they would have found their man playing pool and drinking with all us Tunbridge Wells Chelsea - completely unreal!!!

All us Tunbridge Wells Chelsea had arranged to meet up with the London Chelsea at Dover, so we all left The Kelsey Arms one morning at about 6 am to catch the train to Dover, where we would then get the ferry to Ostend. When we got to Victoria, I noted that West Ham's Intercity Firm were travelling with us to Luxembourg. I turned to Angus and said, "Fuck me Angus, there's going to be a fucking war out there!" I don't think Angus knew what I was on about, because, before we had even left Victoria station for Dover, he was very slightly intoxicated on McEwans. The British Transport police travelled with us on the train all the way to Dover, so there wasn't any trouble on the rattler. When we got to Dover, more police got on, in fact, there were about 200 police especially waiting for us, to travel on the ferry with us to Ostend. I turned to Match and said, "I don't think there will be any trouble until we get to the Belgian match." I was right. The only thing that did happen, was that everyone made their way to the Duty Free shop and bought lots of alcohol, which was drunk before we reached Ostend. When we docked at Ostend, nearly everyone was pissed. The trouble with that was the Belgian authorities had the power to refuse you entry to their country. Some of the younger England fans, travelling with us, were put back on the ferry back to England. 'A lesson learnt'. However, us Tunbridge Wells lads were a bit wiser, and tried to stay sober, until we could get on the train to take us to Brussels. Even Angus had sobered up a bit by now, and he slipped past the huge contingent of Belgian riot police, who were waiting for us at Ostend. The rattler got into Brussels at about 6 am and it was here that we changed trains for Luxembourg. Micky Dunn, Bisal and Paul Gabril were selling T-shirts and flags at the station, whilst waiting for the Luxembourg connection. The younger English fans were buying them, and the selling was going quite well for Sticky and co. A lot of other England fans were sitting around and drinking at the small bar at the station, and eventually the train came into the station for our connection to Luxembourg. I think everyone was glad to see the train, because, by now, people were beginning to get bored with the waiting. The Belgian riot police were also pleased to see the train arrive, and watched us English fans get on it, as they knew we would soon be out of their country without any trouble having been caused. Match, Angus and I walked up and down the carriages, seeing who we could recognise. As I walked along the carriages, I spotted a group of people playing cards and a familiar voice said, "Fancy a hand, Trev?" I looked around to see Sean, Babs and Eccles taking money off some Arsenal fans. I turned to Sean and said, "No thanks, not today!!" We walked on a bit further and found a lot of other Tunbridge Wells Chelsea crashed out on the seats with half empty bottles of Scotch, gin, and wine and cans of lager beside them. I thought to myself, "They won't be awake much before we reach Luxembourg." Then, Match and I bumped into Sticky, Bisal and Paul coming the other way up the train - still flogging their wares! Angus offered me a swig of 'Jack Daniels'. I declined and popped another pill I had acquired from Mr. Warren earlier. I always felt more alive 'speeding up' than getting out of my head on wine, spirits and beer. I still had a taste for the liqueur - it was just that pills and coke worked quicker for me!!

There were quite a few local women on the train, and Match was chatting them up in his usual way. He struck lucky with one of them, and after plying this Belgian lady with wine and chat, he got up from the table and took her to the toilet on the train. He held the door open for her in a very gentlemanly way - there must be something wrong but he followed her in!!! After about ten minutes, they reappeared and Match said to me, "One nil to England, Trev!!"

He then told us how he had had sex with the bird 'doggy' fashion over the toilet. We all thought what a lucky little sod', as the bird was quite tasty, She then sat down next to Match and buttoned up her shirt in front of all of us other lads. Then she and Match carried on drinking as if nothing had ever happened. I thought to myself, 'Nice one Match, that's what I call style!' He had only just met her an hour ago!!

The train pulled into Luxembourg and Andy Warren said to me, "Trev, Angus has collapsed a few carriages up the train, what are we going to do?"

"Fuck knows!" I replied. Then, Match had an idea, there were a lot of luggage trailers on the platform, so we got Angus on to one of them and pushed the trailer past the riot police, who were standing waiting for us English fans. They took one look at Angus and us three pushing him along. The look on their faces said it all - the English lunatics and the cream of English hooligans had arrived!! The doors of the train were slamming open and shut to the chorus of "English boys we are here, we shag your women and drink your beer!!" (Which of course Match had already done, he was always an early starter!) The riot police must have thought to themselves, 'What the fuck are the next couple of days going to be like?' All of the English fans got out of the station pretty safely, apart from a few Northerners, who had decided to take the piss out of the riot police (why, I don't know) and had got a good thumping for their troubles. We managed to get Angus to a local cafe, just outside the station, and we kept supplying him with black coffee until he sobered up. It took a few hours but Angus was one of our own, and he would have done the same for us. It was the law of the jungle, an unwritten hooligan law and certainly a Tunbridge Wells Chelsea law, you see your own safe first! After getting Angus sobered up it was onwards to find a suitable bar to practise our drinking skills. The first bar we went into had a lot of West Ham's Intercity Firm in there, and as we didn't really want to mix with them, we quickly made our excuses and left to find another bar. If they had been fighting any foreign contingent, we would have helped them out, but drinking with them was another matter altogether!! Angus, Match and I were also looking for somewhere to stay, but most of the hotels and guest houses were full, then Match spotted a hotel which had vacancies. We all went in, and asked if there were any rooms available. The woman behind the counter said, "Yes, how many would you like?" Match told her we wanted three rooms, to which she replied, "No problem," she was just about to pass over the keys, when the front door of the hotel burst open and in walked about a dozen Newcastle fans. They had seen us go into the hotel and had followed us in. They were all pissed and were singing and swearing loudly. With that, the woman grabbed back the keys to the rooms and said to us, "No vacancies - we don't want trouble in this hotel." I turned to the Newcastle fans and said, "Thanks a lot, you load of northern wankers! We've just lost rooms in about the only hotel in Luxembourg with vacancies, you tossers!" I don't think they knew what I was saying to them, they were too pissed! But as we were leaving Angus head-butted one of them, just for good measure, and said to him, "Maybe you Northerners want to sleep on the street for a week, but we don't. So, next time you mouth it off, think first, you brainless prats!!" I think they understood what Angus meant! Then I spotted Ian Cox (the jockey), who had also made the trip to Luxembourg. He told us that there were vacancies in the hotel, where he was staying. Luckily for us, they had and we all managed to get rooms and after a quick sleep and a shower, it was back out on the town to find some bars for a good drink up.

There were plenty of tickets available for the match. We didn't even have to bother to look for Sticky or Bisal, because all the newsagents were selling tickets across the counter. Everyone was buying their tickets from the newsagents. A few Scousers were up to their usual thieving tricks, and were nicking fags and other stuff and then running out without paying for it. Luxembourg wasn't exactly Spain, in fact, it was fucking freezing. It was a very dirty place and it didn't seem to have many bars open, which was beginning to piss everyone off. Then this big, fat Belgian bloke came up to us and said, "follow me, lads. All your English pals are drinking in my bar." So, we all followed him to this bar, it wasn't very large but it was packed with English fans and as we walked in a cry went up, "Over here Trev. Where the fuck have you three been?" It was Scranner, Mappe and Connie Butler, local lads from Tunbridge Wells. They flashed a couple of Scotches my way, and I swallowed them in one hit. That soon warmed me up. By this time, the temperature outside was well below freezing. After a fucking good piss up, we all made our way to our hotels feeling nice and warm inside. The next day, the army and the riot police were on the streets, putting on a show of strength, Match and I walked down to the railway station, where English fans were still arriving. We heard that the night before, a plate-glass window in a jewellers shop had been smashed and a load of stuff had been nicked. Apparently, it was down to the Scousers again. Typical Liverpool supporters! I thought why do they do it? Then, a West Ham supporter told us that Hickey was drinking in a certain bar. We went to find him and, sure enough, there he was. We all went into see

105

him,. He said that if England lost the match and didn't qualify, we would have the best fight ever - a fucking war! Next thing I knew, the police and the army were coming into the bar, where we were, and told the owner that it was time to close. We all went out on to the pavement and continued drinking from cans and bottles in the street. The police then told us not to congregate on the street. The situation was beginning to look very ugly, and I thought there was going to be a big off (fight). There must have been about 500 police and army personnel and about 1000 English fans on either side of the road. I then heard the shout, "Sieg-Heil!" and I thought, "Here we go!" but all that happened was that everyone just walked off in different directions. The army and police just didn't know which group to follow, I was standing by some Millwall fans, and they were telling me that they had made plans with West Ham and Arsenal fans to wreck the place, whether England won or lost. The Scousers were also going to use the occasion to do some thieving, and nick a load of gear. The local Luxembourg residents were very scared of the coming night. The police didn't know what to make of us. By now, everyone, was getting pissed and having a good time.

We knew we would easily beat Luxembourg, and we hoped that Greece would help us out by beating Denmark. Outside the ground, Sticky, Bisal and Paul were selling their T-shirts and flags. Poor Bisal didn't make much of a killing that game, as everyone had got their tickets quite easily from the newsagents! Still, I suppose it's a case of 'some you win, some you lose!' All of us Tunbridge Wells had arranged to meet up just outside the ground, and we entered the ground together, under the watchful eye of the riot police inside the ground. The ground was surrounded by barbed wire, and some of the terraces were not open to us fans. They were filled with police just waiting to charge in, at the first sign of trouble. Match, Angus, Andy Warren and I stood behind one of the goals, next to some Millwall fans. One of them had a radio with him, listening to news of the Greece match. As it happens, Denmark scored a couple of goals, so it didn't matter if England won the game here in Luxembourg. We were out. Soon, everybody had heard what was going on in Greece, and the mood on the terraces became violent. England scored two early goals, but it didn't matter to us at all, the trouble started. The Millwall fans next to us joined forces with Arsenal and West Ham fans and started to pull fences down. Then I saw Hickey and some London Chelsea steaming into the West Ham fans, so we all joined forces with Hickey - inter-club rivalries had begun. We were going to have a party, but, because of what had happened in Greece, everyone was getting pissed and smacking the fuck out of each other. Then a cry went up from about a hundred Manchester United fans, "Come on, you cockney bastards, let's have you!"

With that cry from the Northerners hanging over us, the fighting and punch-up between us Head-hunters, West Ham, Millwall and Arsenal fans stopped dead. The main faces of the warring parties shouted to Hickey, "Let's join forces Chels and kick the fuck out of the northern shit and give them a beating they'll never forget!!"

"Right," shouted Steve (Hickey) back, "let's kill them!!" With that, about two hundred Hammers, Gooners, Millwall and Chelsea mentals stormed at the United fans and a massive battle occurred on the terraces. There was blood, guts and Doc-Martins flying into the Man Utd fans from every conceivable angle and position. It was great fun, to say the least, and the Northerners certainly got a lesson in terrace tactics and fighting that day from us southerners, that's for sure! What also sticks in my mind vividly about the occasion and punch-up, was these two fat United supporters who thought they were the main faces of the Man. U. crew. One had 'MUFC' (Manchester United Football Club) tattooed across his forehead and the other had a lot of previous battle scars about his person. One scar went from one ear down to the side of his mouth. It looked like he had been Stanley knifed at some time or another. A couple of right hard bastards they looked, but whether they were the main faces from the Stratford End at Old Trafford, we shall never know. Anyhow, they seemed to know who Hickey was and made a beeline for him. I suppose Hickey's reputation as England's number one hooligan had preceded him, even to northern outposts like Manchester. "Come on you cockney bastards," they kept shouting at Hickey and a few of us others, as they moved up the terrace, closer and evermore menacingly. They now stood about 10 foot from us. They were glaring at us and saying, "You southern softies are all a load of tossers and you're going to get some!!" And just as we were about to launch into each other this voice said, "Southern softies, are we? Take that you northern shit!" and a dozen punches rained down on the Man United mob as quick as a flash, and "Scar Face' fell to the ground like a brick dropping out of the sky. It was Eccles with Babs standing beside him! Fuck knows where he had come from. I knew he was in the ground somewhere but wasn't sure where. He had always had the ability to turn up when you least expected him to, had Danny! As 'Scar Face' hit the ground, the boots went flying into him from other Chelsea, Millwall and West Ham fans and before the other Man United hard nut (with the MUFC tattoo) decided to get lucky, Babs said to him, "Do you fucking want some as well, wanker?" With that, he turned and ran back down the terrace to the safety of his own kind, who by this time were getting a good kicking anyway. So much so for the 'faces' of Manchester United. I thought to myself, "If that's them, forget it!" But deep down I knew that there were some real nutters and hard men from Manchester, not these two jokers. They obviously thought they were the main men, but never in their wildest dreams, would they have expected to meet the original hard man of London terrace violence of that era.

Years later, I was drinking with Babs, Eccles and Sean in The Black Bull in the Fulham Road, just outside Stamford Bridge (Chelsea's home ground). Danny was telling me how on that night in Luxembourg, he was standing at the back of the terrace with Babs and Sean watching the action unfold and "his young Chelsea fight," as he put it when he realised we might have been in a spot of trouble, so he had decided to step in and help. If I ever had to sum up Eccles I would say he was the person we all would have liked to have been. Hickey had taken over from Danny by now, but like a Chinese dynasty, the reins were still really with Danny, it was just that he had let us all have a little more rope to play with. The British Army had Winston Churchill leading them and he was a great leader of men. The biggest tribute I could make to Eccles was that I don't think Churchill could have led us English hooligans abroad any better!!!

When the final whistle went at the end of the game, everybody piled out of the ground. The riot police and the army tried to keep some form of order, but fans just broke into little groups and went everywhere. They didn't know which way to look. Fans were going crazy, throwing bricks through windows and looting shops. Doors were being kicked in, cars were being overturned and anyone who wasn't an England fan was getting punched. The Scousers were breaking any jewellers shop window they could find and nicking watches and gold chains. All signs of reason had gone from their eyes. I saw a couple raiding one particular shop, and they were stashing their ill-gotten gains into a couple of large holdalls. It looked like they were on dope, their eyes were rolling and their tongues were hanging out of the sides of their mouths (like panting dogs!) Perhaps it was just the excitement of the raid, who knows? Others were not so lucky and got nicked by the riot police. Sirens were by now blasting out everywhere and police vans were all around us. The riot police were beginning to search peoples' bags for any stolen goods, but I think they were onto a 'lost cause' as the real culprits had long gone, by the time the police started their searching spree. Windows of shops were still being smashed. Police were still chasing us English fans until the early hours of the morning, and the Scousers were trying to sell the stolen gear to us cockneys. I wondered how they were going to get the nicked gear through customs, and so I asked one of them. He told me that they were going to put it all in the left luggage lockers at the railway station in Ostend, and come back to collect it in a couple of weeks time when all the trouble had died down. Perhaps, Scousers were not as thick as I first thought, but just treated thieving as a hobby and a way to make some money. If one of them got his collar felt by the Old Bill, that was just an occupational hazard.

On the way back to London, Match and I bumped into Sticky, "I'll see you in The Kelsey when you get home." To which he replied, "Yeah, you might, Trev but I've lost my fucking passport!" Anyhow, Sticky and the rest of the heroes made it home as I was reminiscing with him about the trip a week later.

The next match England were to play was against France in Paris. Paris is so easy to get to, so everybody and their wives were going to be there. Match, the General, Hickey, myself and the rest of the Tunbridge Wells and London Chelsea travelled to Paris by ferry from Dover. A lot of heavy drinking was taking place on the ferry. West Ham decided the time was right to have a go at us Chelsea - big mistake! Halfway across the Channel, a massive fight broke out and the ferry got completely wrecked, as there were not any Old Bill about. Bottles and knives were being brandished. Three or four people got stabbed. When the ferry docked, they were taken straight to hospital in France. I recall that during the journey six London Chelsea got hold of two West Ham fans, who were flashing blades and threw them overboard. They went straight in the sea, life jackets and life rings were thrown out to them and they managed to pick them up. I learnt much later that they had both survived. Someone must have been looking after them that day, as they could have so easily drowned. As the ferry docked, the fights simmered down a little. There were quite a few casualties that day from both groups of supporters. I think neither Chelsea or West Ham lost face and that honours were just about even. Personally, I got a bit of a kicking on that journey but that was just a part of the rivalry between us two sets of fans.

When we got to Paris, the French skinheads were waiting for any English fans and attacked us on the Metro. They started to attack us with spray cans containing CS gas - when CS gas is sprayed in confined spaces (like underground carriages) there's nothing you can do, it just overpowers. Chelsea used it when we attacked other supporters, especially the likes of West Ham, Arsenal or Millwall, when we hit the pubs on their home patches.

The fighting continued in the ground, and there were the usual battles and disturbances in the streets - windows were smashed, shops were looted and cars were overturned. The French riot police just looked on in disbelief at us mental English supporters. Amazingly, English fans were still allowed to travel abroad, because the Football Association said that the trouble in Luxembourg and France wasn't as bad as they first thought. However, in my opinion, it was the worst soccer violence perpetrated by English fans that I had ever seen abroad.

# CHAPTER 6

## FROM STAMFORD BRIDGE TO WEMBLEY - NO! FROM THE KELSEY ARMS, TUNBRIDGE WELLS TO MURPHY'S NORTHERN IRELAND!!! - YES

England were due to play Northern Ireland in the next match. After lengthy discussions in The Kelsey with Murphy (the landlord and staunch Irishman), Hickey and the rest of the Tunbridge Wells Chelsea, it was decided that a coach was to be arranged by Hickey to take us to the match. Murphy phoned his brothers and cousins in Northern Ireland to tell them we were going to make the trip over and to pave the way for us. On the last occasion we had gone over to Ireland, we were ambushed by the Northern Irish fans and had taken a severe beating. Murphy assured us all that it would be safe to travel, and that his relatives would get in touch with the well known Northern Ireland 'faces' and make it safe for us, as the Irish fans loved a punch up. It was agreed that the coach would leave from Chelsea and not Tunbridge Wells, this was because the London Chelsea wouldn't have to travel down to Tunbridge Wells. So we all met up in the local watering hole, The Black Bull in the Fulham Road, just down the road from Stamford Bridge. The usual faces were there. Sean, Babs and Eccles sitting in one corner, taking money off all and sundry who cared to sit and join them for a card game. Brixton Charlie, Finney and the Stockwell Chelsea were busy stocking up with cans of lager and bottles of spirits for the long trip to Ireland (and believe, me, if you had ever been on one of Hickey's 'away days' it was usually a long trip, so plenty of liquid refreshment was required). The coach pulled up outside The Black Bull at about ten o'clock at night, and everyone piled on to it, grabbing their seats as quickly as possible. Fuck knows where Hickey got these coaches and drivers from, but the driver must have been about 80 years old if he was a day, but he assured us that he knew the route, so we all settled down for the trip and started opening the cans and bottles.

A Union Jack was draped across the back window with Chelsea Football Club written on it in big white letters, just to let everyone know who we were, we also put flags in the side windows. The coach looked like the one in the film 'The Italian Job'. Hickey sat at the front of the coach giving orders and taking control of the so-called 'stereo' system. Everyone was singing along to the Rolling Stones and The Beatles, as the coach pulled away from the Fulham Road on route to Holyhead and Dublin. Various stops were made on the way. The first was the obligatory 'beer stop' at an off licence to stock up on beer, fags and food. Hickey advised us not to get caught if we had to nick stuff as we had to make the connection at Holyhead for the Dublin ferry (we were already running behind schedule). Still, with Ayrton Senna at the wheel of the coach we should make it with time to spare!! Oh Yeah!!! Then we stopped in Arsenal territory (North London) to pick up a couple of Murphy's relatives, who were going to use our trip as an excuse to visit relatives in Northern Ireland, and also to go to the match themselves. We also made an unscheduled stop at a motorway service station on the M1 to pick up a couple of Hickey's mates, who I didn't recognise from the terraces at Chelsea. Hickey later informed me that they were National Front leaders, and they wanted to show their Loyalist brothers in Northern Ireland that they would not give into the IRA. Anyhow, that's what Hickey told me, I didn't really understand all that stuff about Ireland, and I still don't. Come to that, I didn't want to know - football was my crack (and still is), and if Ireland and the IRA have a problem, then, in my view, they should be left to sort it out between themselves, but Hickey seemed to be interested in it all! There was a lot of 'National Front' literature distributed on the coach for us punters to read, but Angus, Match, Mr Warren and I couldn't be arsed with it and we carried on drinking and getting merry.

We eventually reached Holyhead at about ten o'clock in the morning, the ferry was due to leave at about one o'clock in the afternoon, so we had made it with a couple of hours to spare. The ferry crossing to Ireland was pretty uneventful, apart from a couple of little fights, but this was just down to football disagreements and nothing major. The next morning the ferry docked in Dublin and we all piled back on the coach again. We went straight through customs. Everyone was well knackered by this time and was catching up on their sleep. After a couple of hours driving, the inevitable happened, the fucking coach conked out. This was always happening on 'away days' with Hickey's coaches, so no one took any notice. The old driver just got his tool box out from under his seat to try and fix the problem. After about an hour, the driver got back in and started up the coach and off we went again. Belfast here we come!!! We went straight through the army border crossing with no trouble. In fact, I think the people at the crossings and checkpoints were amazed to see a coach load of 'mentals' from England travelling to Belfast for a football match. When we eventually got to Belfast, the coach stopped outside a big hotel. I'll always remember it, because it had large lumps of metal sheeting around it, because it had been bombed on a few occasions. The hotel reminded me of something you would see in the Bronx in America - a kind of metal fortress. The security situation in Northern Ireland had eased a little by this time. Murphy's relatives were telling me that the checkpoints were still there, but they were now unmanned. They suggested a pub we should use as a meeting place called Robinson's and that was where the coach was to pick us up after the game. I was still putting two and two together and getting five - Sean O'Callaghan (The Jackal), the bombing of the Grand Hotel, the connections with Murphy and, now, his brothers were telling us where it was safe for us to go. Had I unwillingly entered into something I didn't really understand, just because I followed England and Chelsea? I never found out the answer, but if I put my hand on my heart, I think us lads from The Kelsey were, in some small way, unwittingly getting involved in something far more sinister than football violence. A year of so later, The Kelsey Arms was burnt to the ground and had to be rebuilt from scratch. Read into that what you will, but I think you'll probably come up with the same answer as I did.

My view of the situation is as follows: football violence is a way of life - but give Ireland back to the Irish - it's as simple as that!! Within a couple of hours of the coach arriving in Belfast, one of the blokes from the National Front got nicked by the Royal Ulster Constabulary. Hickey told me he had got nicked, because he had been caught giving out leaflets detailing the way the National Front worked and recruited its members. Hickey also said that no National Front badges were to be worn in the pubs and bars in the part of Belfast we were in, and if the RUC caught anyone with 'Front' literature they would be nicked. I got talking to Murphy's relative Sean (another Irish Sean, but not of The Jackal variety!) and he told me that all the people at the match who supported Northern Ireland, would all be staunch Loyalists. He assured us that this would prevent them from beating us English fans up.

He told me that the last time England played Northern Ireland in Belfast, the Old Bill had let the English fans make their own way back through the town after the match. An that all the Irish had come out of the bars and clubs and, murdered, any of the English they could lay their hands on. After he had told me this, I began to wish I was back in The Kelsey drinking with his cousin Mick, the landlord. But Sean again assured me that we were safe all the time he was with us!

None of us had any match tickets which was a problem. Everyone was saying that there were no 'spares' and that the touts didn't have any, I thought that if I could have found Sticky or Bisal, I might have been able to get a couple of tickets. However I didn't know where they were and I couldn't get in touch with them. They had made their own way to Belfast! Murphy's cousins, Sean and Paddy introduced us lads from Tunbridge Wells to some more of their relatives. They were also great people, very friendly and hospitable. Hickey then decided he wanted to go for a walk down to the Falls Road (a Catholic area of Belfast) but Murphy's cousins warned him not to go down there. Hickey being Hickey said to me, "Come on, Trev,. I've got a taxi. Let's go and have a look around." So, Hickey, Match, Angus and I piled into a taxi and asked to be taken to the Falls Road. We had heard that many drivers would not drive down there, but this chap didn't seem to mind taking our money, so off we went! Belfast to me seemed like any other large European city, apart from the murals on the walls of buildings and houses. I remember one particular house had the words, "Cowardly Loyalist Backout' painted on it. Sean later explained to me that it was about the struggle for freedom, and the Loyalist paintings in the Shankhill estates that were in total contrast as they depicted solidarity with the mainland. I also remember the army barracks at the bottom of the Falls Road had gigantic concrete walls sloping outwards at the top, which was against mortar attacks. It looked to me like a prison. By this time, we had had enough of our tour of Belfast so the taxi driver took us back to the safe haven of Robinson's bar. Murphy's relatives gave us a bollocking for going down the Falls Road without them. I think they saw themselves as our guardian angels in Belfast. I was glad as I felt relatively safe being in their company. I went up to the bar and bought a round of drinks for all of Murphy's relatives, much as a 'bonding' exercise, but also, because they were good people and we had come to rely on them a bit for our safety whilst in Belfast. They sat with us Tunbridge Wells lads for most of the evening, telling us tales of Murphy and of 'old' Ireland and singing Irish ballads. We were all getting pissed on 'the black stuff', which they seemed to handle quite easily but for us cockneys was a struggle to drink, not a bit like lager. A lot of the other lads decided that they also wanted to take a look down the Falls Road, after hearing Hickey's tales of what it was like. About half a dozen of them decided to go for a walk but they didn't get as far as we got in the taxi, and they were turned back for their own safety by the RUC.

Most of the Irish fans that I spoke to had tickets for the match, and they also said that we wouldn't be able to purchase any. I said to Angus and Match, "Let's go down to the ground to see if we can get any tickets there." So, off we set (With Sean in close attendance) on the walk to the ground. The RUC were in evidence everywhere. They all carried Stun guns and large truncheons. I thought to myself, "I don't fancy getting on the wrong side of them!' The walk to the ground took about an hour. Once we got there, we started asking if anyone had any spare tickets. Match asked one young Irishman, who promptly told him, "I would rather set fire to them than give them to any fucking Englishman!" I could see Match getting angry by this comment, but Sean told him not to say or do anything as it could turn nasty. For once in his life, Match took Sean's advice and the situation died down, thank God!!!

Then, I heard another Irish voice, it was Sean's brother Paddy who said, "Still looking for tickets, Trev?"

"Of course I am!" I replied, to which he said, "I've got thirty of them!" and he had. Christ knows where he had got them from. "How much?" I asked.

"As you're Murphy's mates - face value, I don't want to make a killing, Trev." I couldn't believe my luck because the tickets were like gold dust. All us lads on the coach got tickets.

England won 1-Nil. The Irish fans left the match a little early. The RUC stopped English fans leaving at the same time. They had decided to escort the English fans who had travelled by rail back to the station. The Irish fans were walking right up to the RUC (who were trying to protect the English) and were throwing punches and spitting at the opposition, the RUC were having to struggle with the Irish fans. Angus, Andy Warren, Match and myself were still standing on the terraces. I decided to take a look out in the car park to see what was happening. I looked out and saw about a hundred Irish fans waiting for us. I went back to the lads and told them what I had seen. Angus said, "Trev, I expect we're going to get a fucking good kicking. Here, have some whisky!" This was Angus's answer to everything. On this occasion, I was thinking he might just be wrong and whisky wasn't the answer. By this time, we were surrounded by about another fifty English fans, who must have seen us as some sort of safe haven for an escape from the ground. The next thing I knew, Sean and Paddy had come back into the ground - "Follow me!" Sean shouted and we did! "Was he leading us to a good beating or safety?" I asked myself. We all followed Sean and Paddy like sheep out of the ground and into the car park. Sean said to me, "Trev, don't even blink an eyelid and stay close!" I was not about to question him! The Irish crowd in the car park had grown to about two thousand and they were looking for any excuse to fight and maim any English fans, but we felt safe with Sean and Paddy. Ten minutes later, the RUC began to beckon the English fans over to where they were. Our group were in the front, along with the other Chelsea and West Ham fans. The walk back to our coach pick-up point took us through streets with 'Coronation Street' style houses on both sides. The Irish had no fear of us English fans. Getting nicked didn't bother them, they just stood around the streets ready for a fight - then it started. I saw Hickey, Babs and Eccles going in first and we all followed. Soon, there was a massive battle going on. This gigantic Irish bloke went at Angus with a lump of wood and cracked him right over the head with it. Blood spurted everywhere, but I don't think Angus felt it too much as he was quite pissed. On seeing this happen, I picked up a house brick, that I had found in the street to use as a weapon, and smacked it right in this Irishman's face, screaming at the top of my voice, "Take that, you Irish scum!" Again, blood went everywhere and he fell to the ground like a bag of shit. Next thing I knew, some West Ham fans were helping us, and getting us out of the situation. We all escaped into the darkness of the night, with the blood still pouring from Angus's battle wound. By this time, he had a couple of football scarves wrapped around his head, and the flow of blood was easing a little. It was a couple of days later after he had some stitches put in the wound, that it began to look any better. He looked a right mess for months later, poor old Angus!

We still had a long way to go to the pick-up point and there were a lot of mad, angry Irishmen still about on the streets looking to give a good beating to any English fans they could find. As we turned one corner, a group of about twenty to thirty Irish fans were coming the other way. They spotted we were English fans straight away and started to run at us shouting, "You're going to fucking die, you English dogs!" We had nowhere to turn, so we just had to stand there and fight, and fight we did! I hit one of the Irishmen with a lucky punch straight in the head, and, as he went down, Match and Angus put the boot in. Suddenly, I was being pulled backwards with a truncheon across my head by four RUC officers. They threw me up against an armoured Range Rover, and then a couple of them started to hit me with their truncheons across the back and legs. The pain was unbelievable, it felt like I had been run over by a bus. The RUC sergeant had his hand around my neck and pinned me up against a wall and said to me, "That will teach you a lesson, you English bastard! If I see you causing anymore trouble, we won't be here for you, we'll let the Irish fans deal with you, now fuck off!" I could hardly walk and I was stumbling around, I was very unsteady on my feet. I have had a few beatings and kickings in my time from rival fans on the terraces and streets, but I had never had a beating like that before in my life, and I never want to get one again!!! In fact, I didn't find out until I got back to England that I had broken two ribs. I discovered this when I went for a check-up at my local hospital, because I was still in so much pain from our trip to Ireland.

I couldn't wait to get back to Hickey's coach and get some rest and also get back to Dublin, as it was my escape route back to England. Angus was still with me and kept giving me shots of whisky to dull the pain from the beating. We rounded another corner, and some more Irish fans came at us, and I got smacked straight in the head. By this time, I was feeling too weak to fight back and just fell to the ground. Luckily, Angus was still next to me and hit the Paddy over the head with the whisky bottle we were drinking from. After seeing this happen the other Irish fans began to back off a bit. The RUC were still about and spotted what was happening and moved in to try and protect Angus and me. They told us to stop where we were. The Irish fans stood on the other side of the road, still baying at us and a small group of English fans, who had joined us for safety. They were shouting, "You're going to die, you fucking English pigs!" One of the other English lads with us, who had seen me being pulled up and beaten by the RUC, said to me, "You've taken the beating of your life, mate. We're Arsenal and we'll get you back to your coach." I found out later that he was one of the leaders of the Gooners, Arsenal's main firm. Angus and I were certainly glad he was around with a few of his crew. When he found out we were Chelsea, we both thought they would all leave us to our own devices, but they just said to us, "No matter what our differences are at home, you're English mates, and we'll get you and your mates through this, Chels."

I now look at Arsenal fans in a different light whenever we play them at the Bridge or at Highbury. Months later, I was speaking to Eccles in The Black Bull and reminiscing about the Irish trip and my exploits with Angus. Eccles said to me, "I know all about it Trev, I was speaking to Johnny Hoy (the leading face at Arsenal) the other evening on the phone, about arranging to hit the Yids (Tottenham), and he told me about you and Angus." It always amazes me how quickly terrace gossip gets around, especially, from the leading faces of different London clubs. Everyone seems to know exactly what's happening (or about to happen), well, Eccles and Hickey always seem to know!! I suppose that's one of the reasons they are leaders and number one on the terraces.

The Irish supporters were still everywhere and were following us along the roads. They kept shouting and spitting at us and telling us that if it wasn't for the Old Bill, then we would be dead. The RUC kept trying to move them on, but the Irish didn't take any notice of them. I expect that arrests were kept to a minimum, because the authorities didn't have the time to go to court over things like GBH or football related matters. Suddenly, the RUC told us to stand still, I wondered why? Then, there was a great explosion. It was a bomb going off in the distance, the noise shook the ground we were standing on. I've never experienced anything like that before. It was a very scary feeling. After the explosion, we were told to move on again by the RUC. The Irish were still following us, but were a bit further away from us. By this time I was feeling a little safer, as we were now being joined by more English supporters and more RUC men.

A fleet of British Army armoured cars flew past with sirens going. All the English fans cheered. We reached the end of this particular street, and most of the English fans who had travelled over by train and ferry were escorted by the RUC to the railway station. Our little group walked back down the road to Robinson's bar with about six RUC men protecting us. We also had an armoured Land Rover moving alongside us for protection as well!!! As we were walking past one pub, we were shouted at, "Come back, you English dogs, and fight like men!" We wanted to break ranks and fight, but we knew that if we did, the RUC would be powerless to protect us, and that, in this situation, someone might be killed. We managed to get to Robinson's bar safely. We were told to stay inside the bar. We were to stay and wait for the coach to pick us up. "Sound advice," I thought to myself. Some Millwall and Arsenal fans decided against the advice of the RUC, and went back out on to the streets to see if they could find some Irish for a punch-up. We never saw them again, so I don't know what happened to them, I can only assume that they made their own way back to the mainland safely.

So that was our trip to Ireland over with. "Thank Christ!" I thought to myself. I was glad to get back on Hickey's coach and get out of Belfast that night, I can tell you! The Irish fans are a tough crowd and well worth their salt in a fight. They are very strong and are not scared of anything.

Just outside London at Mill Hill, the coach broke down. The driver got out to try and fix it, but we all got off and caught the tube into Central London and left him to it. So, that was the Irish trip and one of Hickey's 'away days' over. I've always thought that England 'away days' are much better fun than home games, because you always bump into old adversaries and there is a camaraderie amongst the people who travel abroad, which is hard to find at home. A lot of nonsense has been written about Hickey by people who don't know him. As previously mentioned, we both graduated from The Roebuck to The Kelsey to The Black Bull, and I saw him rise from the obscurity of a mere 'Shed' boy to a terrace leader and legend at Chelsea. Us lads from 'the Wells' all admired him for that. Hickey was a great travel organiser of 'away days'. He learnt his trade very early on from the General and me on our various outings in transit vans to away grounds, setting off from The Roebuck to all points of the country. He was never a vicious thug, but could handle himself in a fight, that was for sure. When Hickey spoke, people listened to what he had to say. He had a certain aura about him, which you usually find in a VIP. I think because of his reputation, people liked to be seen with him. If he spoke to you, it gave you instant 'street cred'. He is known at every football ground in the country. His reputation secured him a sort of folk hero status, a sort of Sir Bob Geldof of the football terraces! If medals were awarded for football terrace violence, Hickey would have been first in line for one, that I'm sure of.

Hickey was arrested just before Easter 1986. His arrest made the national press and the television news. The police put on a display of the weapons supposedly used on the terraces for soccer violence. I couldn't believe it, when I saw what was being shown. There was one weapon which looked like a medieval ball and chain, and there were large swords and lances. What a load of bollocks!!

Hickey's hobby was collecting medieval weapons. He was always buying stuff like this from the local junk shops in Tunbridge Wells and Brighton. But the Old Bill were trying to say he was using them on the terraces - utter rubbish, but they were trying to pin this on him. The police operation was called 'Own Goal' and a news team were invited to film it, so much for innocent until proven guilty, this law seems to apply to everyone except football fans. The main problem for Hickey was that he had become a well known terrace face, and the Old Bill were always looking for him at away grounds. He was also beginning to let anyone go on his 'away day' travels. He saw it as a way to make more profit. There were always plenty of nutters on the coaches, not a lot of brains between them, but they could handle themselves in a fight. All the police had to do, was to observe the away fans at football matches. They could easily pick out the leaders. I think us Chelsea lads were definitely picked on, Hickey in particular. I think it was because Hickey had such a large following, not only in this country, but around the world at England games. There was also talk that the National Front were sponsoring foreign trips for England fans to help spread their beliefs, but I don't think that was true.

The Black Bull in the Fulham Road, just outside Stamford Bridge, where we drank before Chelsea games, was always packed with nutters that followed Chelsea, and, it was where Hickey and the rest of us Tunbridge Wells fans drank, it was well patronised. It was our local at Chelsea and nobody dared go in unless they were Chelsea faces, one time two plain-clothes constables came into the pub dressed as Chelsea supporters. They had been seen in the Chelsea Shed on a few occasions, so they were welcomed as being Chelsea 'Shedites'. Nobody thought that they were the Old Bill. We were being infiltrated and didn't even know it! They started travelling on the coaches with us, gaining information and compiling dossiers about us, Hickey in particular. We thought they were just a couple more Chelsea nutters joining the firm. How wrong can you be! The bastards!! When Hickey was arrested, his trial was predictable. It all rested on what the two plain-clothes constables had seen happening at away grounds and terraces around the country. How the jury believed them!! The police made out that Hickey was the reason why there was always trouble on the terraces at England matches. Yes, he was definitely a leading face in the world of terrace aggro, but never the main cause of it. After all, Hickey was our mate, so how could he be? I thought the ten years sentence Hickey got was completely unfair and unjust. After a few years in prison, Hickey's brief got him out. The story goes that the Old Bill had fabricated evidence against Hickey and a few others, and the case against Hickey was dropped. He got a substantial out-of-court settlement for his lost years. I could never understand the length of his sentence, not even bank robbers or rapists serve that amount of time inside nick. I just think they wanted to make an example of him, but in the end it didn't work, and the Old Bill were left with 'egg on their faces'. British justice, it was a farce, it applies to everyone except football fans!!

I remember another occasion when Chelsea were in the old second division. The General, Hickey, Eccles and I were all drinking in the bar of the old Chelsea West stand, and we were talking about how we were going to 'hit' Millwall's Bushwackers when they came to the Bridge to play Chelsea in a couple of weeks time. Hickey, as per usual, was organising the route Millwall would take to get to Chelsea, and where it would be best to surprise them for a fight. The rest of us were planning tactics and how many Chelsea 'Shedites' we needed for the punch-up. The last time Millwall had visited the Bridge they thought they had run and beaten Chelsea. In fact, all they had done was to scare a few dozen Chelsea youngsters who were walking along the Fulham Road.

They hadn't reckoned on us 'known' faces surprising them from all directions, as we all came out of 'The Nell Gwynne', 'The Weavers' and 'The Black Bull' pubs. Millwall didn't know what had hit them that day, as we fought and ran them from every direction imaginable. That day was certainly Chelsea's but I can recall going to Coldharbour Lane (The Den, Millwall's old gound) and in the early years Millwall ran Chelsea from the terraces. Mind you, I was only about fifteen years of age, but the sight of all those burly, scar-faced dockers running over the railway sleepers, that in those day were called terraces, certainly put the fear of God up a young Garb, Pete Jefferys and myself, I can tell you!!

Garb, Hickey, Babs, Eccles and I were drinking in the bar of the old West stand at Chelsea and planning for Millwall in a couple of week's time. It was about 2.30 in the afternoon and kick off for the match was at 3 pm. The disc jockey was playing records and announcing requests around the ground over the loudspeakers. All of a sudden, the music stopped and the disc jockey said, "I have a special request from Dave (Smiler) Jones from Millwall," who was one of Millwall's leaders at the time. He went on to say, "He says hello to Hickey, Babs, Eccles, Sean and co. and hopes the reception they are preparing for him and Millwall will be better than the last time Chelsea met Millwall, as that was very disappointing!" We all looked at each other and burst out laughing there was also stunned silence at the cheek of it! But, if he and his 'bushwackers' want a special welcome, they were sure to get a very warm one now, after a wind up like that!

Most clubs had their crews and firms. We at Chelsea were known as the 'Head-hunters' and we used to leave a card after a fight, this was copied by the West Ham firm who called themselves the 'Intercity Firm' Arsenal were the 'Gooners', Millwall were the 'Bushwackers', Spurs were called the, Yiddos', Leeds were the 'Service Crew' and the craziest of all had to be Birmingham who called themselves the 'Zulu Warriors'.

During my time supporting Chelsea and England, I have made a lot of friends and met a lot of people of a like mind from all over the country. Some have stayed friends for life, even though they support a different club to me. I would never fight them and vice versa. On a cold night, in a northern outpost, on a rain sodden street, with the opposition fans just about to give you a kicking, you learn more about human behaviour than you ever would on a five-year college course. I think people and politicians in government in particular, don't understand football thugs and hooligans. I would love to take these people in so-called 'high places' to a football match one day, just so that they could see first hand what life on the terraces is all about. They could experience it for themselves and hopefully try and understand it all. Most of the people I know at football have mundane jobs, Monday to Friday, 7.30 to 5.00 and look forward to Saturdays, because Saturday is their day to be somebody. They can let all their pent up feelings go on the terrace with a fight or punch up, wreck a train or cause havoc in a town. It allows them to be someone else for a short time. They gain respect from their fellow supporters and mates. People tell me that football hooliganism is not as bad as it was a few years ago, and perhaps that's correct, but being on the inside of it, I totally disagree. I know that if there's to be trouble at a match, the same faces are involved, who were involved five, ten, even fifteen years ago. Believe me, soccer violence is still there and very much alive. Police video cameras, 'all seater' stadia and better police organisation make it a lot harder for a good old fashioned punch-up nowadays, it is now much more of an organised violence.

A quick attack on the opposition's pub, or hit the opposition well away from their grounds and get out fast, is what it's all about today. Most grounds are now like prisons, all caged in. All the Old Bill have done is to transfer the violence away from the main ground. Violence can now erupt anywhere and at anytime, unlike the 'old days', when a goal was scored or a penalty given against your team, this was the green light for a fight on the terraces. The Old Bill used to stop and watch the fighting until it quietened down, then, they would move into the warring parties with their truncheons swinging and hit people indiscriminately. Oh Happy times!!! I don't ever think we will see the return of those days. It's a shame, that's my view, anyway. When I first got involved in terrace violence a good punch-up was normal on a Saturday afternoon. It was, if you like, a sort of apprenticeship to the world of soccer hooliganism. There were definitely more punch-ups between rival fans when I was younger than there are nowadays. Occasionally, you would hear of a blade being used. This was usually done with a Stanley knife, a very vicious and nasty weapon. Nowadays, every fight seems to end with a stabbing or someone getting seriously injured or maimed. I don't really know why this is. I have always looked upon someone who uses a knife as being a bit of a coward. My opinion is, if you can't use your fists when you are confronted by the rival fans, then don't bother. I have seen first-hand, blades used at football matches on rival fans. But, it is a fact of life now. It's the society we now live in. I firmly believe, that anyone who is caught by the police using a knife at football matches, should be sent down straight away, and spend a long time in prison. Knives and stabbings are not what terrace violence is all about and never has been. Locking an offender up would make them think about what they have done. When they are finally released from prison they hopefully would never use a knife again on another individual. I am writing this from the heart because I know of someone who lost their life due to being stabbed.

Everyone has their own ideas but football reflects the way we live, it is certainly true of a lot of the younger generation of this country. There has always been violence at football grounds. Youngsters see it as a way to make themselves heard. In fact, they consider their behaviour perfectly acceptable. People in Government hate hooligans, which I can totally understand. But just picture this, the House of Lords are respectable, responsible people, shouting, abusing, and sometimes assaulting each other - are we really that much apart? Is there that much difference between a soccer hooligan and a Member of Parliament? At least, at Chelsea we used to cheer the rival fans - well sometimes anyway!!! Football hooliganism is no way as bad nowadays as it was when I was a terrace apprentice, but it is still there simmering just under the surface, ready to raise it's ugly head again, and from time to time it does. Yes, I suppose you could say soccer violence is diminishing at English grounds. Hooligans and thugs now go to Europe, where a good old fashioned fight and punch-up is not so much frowned upon as it is at home. It also gives the hooligans the chance to travel abroad and fill up on wines, beers and spirits and cause mayhem in foreign capitals without the fear of a long jail sentence, if they happened to get nicked for causing trouble and football related offences.

I think it's a mixture of sun, beer, travel and foreign women that make a hooligan want to go abroad (and of course the fighting and havoc they can cause) and last of all, the football, but not necessarily in that order! My biggest concern is there's no way of stopping trouble in foreign locations, so English fans will always get bad press. I suppose the people in authority could try taking every England supporter's passport off them when travelling, but how would the law impose that? Who's an England fan and who isn't an England fan? The police know the well known faces but we still travel, so I cannot see that course of action ever being implemented. Or, what about when England play on foreign soil, that country's army could shepherd the England fans in and out of their country but surely that's already been tried and failed. I really don't know what the answer is? There's always going to be drunken English behaviour with the younger England supporters abroad. They tend to see it as an 'away day' holiday, a chance to match their wits and fight against foreign hooligans. Whenever England are playing Germany, 'God save the Queen' is sung at full voice, just to remind the Germans that we won the war. It winds them right up! I think that a lot of England fans when travelling abroad, see themselves as followers of Winston Churchill and have got to fight for England's 'green and pleasant land' no matter what, thinking, 'We'll show the 'Krauts' who's best, and show them why they lost the last war.' The Government and politicians are not really interested in football and it's supporters, unless they can get their names in the papers and gain publicity out of a situation for themselves. Sometimes an MP might go to a big game such as an England match or the FA Cup Final, but football for most Members of Parliament is something that damages the English reputation abroad. They don't seem to care that millions of young Englishmen get fantastic enjoyment from the game. The Government have taken a lot of money in tax from football and put very little back into the game. Admittedly, some grounds are a lot better than when I was younger, but a lot of that is down to the club's chairman and not the Government. Take for instance my own club, Chelsea, if it had not been for the foresight of our own Chairman, Mr Ken Bates in the early 80's, Stamford Bridge would be a right mess of a ground. Now, when I go to the Bridge it's like walking through the gates of heaven, but no thanks to the Government. I might not agree with some of Ken Bates's principles and opinions but he made Stamford Bridge what it is today. I bet you that if the football terraces were where all the political action was, things would be a lot different and so would the response from the politicians. When Ken Bates walked into Stamford Bridge in 1982 to take over the Chairman's role from Brian Mears, he had a vision. It has been a long, hard slog, with many setbacks along the way, but like I say, it is now a pleasure to go to The Bridge, even though I don't like 'all seater' stadia. During Ken Bates's time as Chairman of Chelsea Football Club, there has been a number of significant steps: stopping Cabra Estates in their fight to evict Chelsea from their ancestral home and obtaining security of tenure in 1992; Starting the building of the North stand in 1993; The Matthew Harding saga, which started off so well but then degenerated into a forlorn power struggle and ended in tragedy; The Flotation of the club in 1996 and the subsequent raising of £38.2 million of new capital; £75 million Eurobond issue in 1997, (the first of any sporting club in the world); And, probably the most significant step of all, the strategic alliance signed with BSkyB in the year 2000. That increased Chelsea's share capital to nearly £72 million and net assets to well over £100 million. Mr Bates's 'game plan' has been consistent throughout, dash for growth, complete the development as quickly as possible and strengthen the football team to complete at the highest level with some of Europe's elite. And, during all this, did the Government ever help or put their hands in their well lined pockets and put back some of the money taken from tax generated by football. No!!!! It was all done by Ken, and at Chelsea we have him to thank for that. And we have a certain Mr Tony Banks, MP who confesses to being a lifelong Chelsea fan, a politician and Government figure, celebrity status, I think so! Like I said earlier, politicians are not really interested in football, football clubs and the people who follow them, unless they gain some publicity out of it. I bet they don't know the names of the current players in the team, as they just go to matches for drinks and prawn sandwiches and to sit with their high-powered friends chatting in a box in corporate seating, not caring what is happening down on the pitch. Enough said!!!

Oh yes, and what about the comment from ex-Prime Minister Maggie Thatcher, she was really on the ball, wasn't she? She said, "Why can't the game be played behind closed doors and be relayed via television?" Christ, what planet did that woman come from? And she was running the country at that time, what hope is there for the rest of us? Someone pointed out to her that if this were the case there would be no point in playing football at all. I think anyone with so little understanding of the game and no real knowledge of football ought not to be involved in its control and legislation, but she was!! God help us all!!

Football is a fantastic game and I love it and will always do so. The time and era that I lived through on the terraces was, without doubt, the best days of my life (wife and family excluded). It brought me many 'lows', but the laughs cancelled them out easily. I would not have swapped it for anything. The people from the terraces, mates and foes, all feel the same, I'm sure of that. I look back with great affection at a very special period of time in my life. There were times when I was so scared, I wished that the ground would open up so I could disappear, but I lived to tell the tale. There were also a lot of times when it seemed like I was the luckiest and happiest person in the world. The best times of my life, definitely. Sheer bliss!!! (Well, sometimes). I wouldn't have changed anything, a special time and a magical era.

Everyone has an opinion on football hooligans and terrace violence. The Government, newspaper reporters, who's right?? I don't know the answer to that question, but what I do know is this, that I have written this book from a terrace fan and hooligan's view-point. I would never class myself as an out and out thug or nutter of the violent kind. I was never the sort of fan who would go to a match with the sole intention of hurting someone, the sort of person who enjoyed slashing someone with a knife or kicking someone repeatedly, when they were down on the ground. Although I always liked a good fight on the terraces against the opposition on a Saturday. That was a completely different thing to the 'nutters' code of conduct. I have written the facts as I saw them during my time on the terraces, following England and Chelsea. I have tried not to glorify the violence. The people in this book are real life people, and most of them are still my mates, who I could rely on in any situation and that makes me proud. I hope I have shared the situations and excitement of life on the terraces with whoever reads this book. I suppose some people will say 'That's not how it happened' but through my mind's eye it's exactly how it happened. (Ask anyone who drinks or drank in 'The Imperial', 'Nell Gwynne', 'Rising Sun', 'Wheatsheaf', 'Adelaide' and especially 'the Black Bull').

I hope that when I finally leave this mortal coil, my memories of Utopia will still be with me. That is how I saw my youth, spent following England and Chelsea Football Club. From the first moment, Garb and myself set foot on that old, rickety terrace with its metal roof, which Micky Greenaway and the Webb brothers nicknamed the Shed, I knew I had found my heaven and home and so did Garb (the General). The singing and chants used to echo from the old tin roof. Everyone was packed in like sardines, so tight, swaying forward when Chelsea attacked or scored a goal, or if any trouble started. It was a brilliant era, even if you did have to put up with someone near you pissing up your leg, it just didn't seem to matter at the time. From the Shed we all graduated to the North Stand, Gate 13, so we could mingle with the 'away' supporters and run them off our patch whenever we felt like it, or if Babs or Danny told us to do so. Then it was the old West Stand, with its bar and warm beer, (some things never change at Chelsea). Nowadays, most of the early 'faces' are season ticket holders and only get involved if needs be. I saw Danny (Eccles) a few months ago in one of the bars at Stamford Bridge, created by Ken Bates, and he was still holding court, chatting with a new crop of youngsters. He still had a certain aura about him that you would only probably get from some famous rock star, VIP or famous footballer, a living legend and true gentleman. He will definitely go down in Chelsea folklore. I think Mr Bates should name a bar after Eccles. I have written to him to ask him if he would agree to do this. Unfortunately, I am still awaiting a reply to my letter. He probably threw my letter straight in the bin and sat in his big office thinking, 'Another letter from a Chelsea nutter.' If only Ken knew how much money Eccles and the likes of Babs and Hickey have brought through the Stamford Bridge turnstiles during their time, he might, just for once, come down from his 'ivory tower' to street level and give someone that deserves it, a little bit of recognition. 'Eccles's Bar' has a certain ring about it. Us loyal Chelsea fans would certainly see Mr Bates in a more human light, then. Yes, the terraces may have gone and with them a lot of the atmosphere and passion, but outside in the pubs and clubs around the ground it still lives on and always will!!

# CHAPTER 7

## STOCKHOLM

Another weekend over with, another boring week of work ahead. Oh well, I suppose the pennies have got to come in from somewhere to keep the wolf from the door, I was thinking to myself, "Cup of tea, Trev?" said my mate who I was working with at the time, when, all of a sudden, my mobile went off. A voice at the other end said, "Trev, get your arse down here to Baldwin's (our local travel agency in Tunbridge Wells) we're going to Stockholm tomorrow for the game on Wednesday!" It was Match and the game in question was the final of the European Cup Winners Cup between Chelsea and the Germans - VFB Stuttgart. I quickly made my excuses at work, and as I had a few days holiday left to take, I was gone and was straight down to the travel agents. I was greeted by Micky Dunn, Match, Jeff Moss and Besa sorting out coupons that they had been saving from the national newspapers so that they could get cheap flights to European destinations. After a couple of hours of completely confusing the young lady behind the jump (desk), we had our tickets with Ryan Air to fly the following day from Stansted to Sweden. Good old Sticky had saved up lots of these coupons that were needed for the cheap flights on the 'no frills' aircraft. But what did that matter? I was just about to experience the greatest week in my Chelsea life. A few pounds were exchanged for each ticket - about £90 each (as I remember) and our passports shown and we were all ready to go. It was left to Sticky to arrange the times and further details of our travels and the following morning, we all set off to Stansted Airport from The Kelsey Arms car park in a mini bus, that Sticky had hired from a local taxi firm. All the swag was loaded on the bus (flags and T-shirts) ready to be sold in Stockholm, and just as the dawn was breaking over Tunbridge Wells that Tuesday morning, we moved off.

The cans of lager and bottles of spirits were being opened and consumed to the tune of 'Stockholm Stockholm, here we come' and it was still only 5.30 am, but what the fuck, this was going to be a once in a lifetime trip. I knew that in my own mind, and in my heart I hoped this was going to be Chelsea's finest moment. So I was straight onto the booze. The mood was set for the rest of the trip. Whatever was going to happen from now on, I knew I wouldn't have a lot of control over it. It was going to be in the hands of the gods (carefree). At about 7.30am the mini-bus pulled into the car park at Stansted, and we all got out with suitcases full of T-shirts and flags. Some of us made our way to get something to eat, while others headed straight to the airport bar for liquid refreshments! By this time, more and more Chelsea were turning up at the airport terminal, and old friendships were being renewed, and tales and stories were being swapped of previous encounters. The flight to Sweden was due to take off at midday, so there was plenty of drinking time to be had. As Ryan Air was a cheap, no frills airline, we all knew there wouldn't be any drinks on the plane, so now seemed to be a good a time as ever to stock up for the trip. Sticky, Match, Angus, Jeff Moss, Besa and myself were joined on the trip over to Sweden by Paul Gabril and Paul Baitup, who were going to help Sticky sell the swag in Stockholm. Andy Warren was also with us, but Andy being Andy was out of his head already on lager and Coke (up his nose), so it was decided to try and sober him up, as they might not let him on the plane, and he would miss the fun. Another local person on the trip was Darren, a full-blooded Shedite, his dad Richard is also a complete Chelsea nutter. Richard and his wife Christine run another pub in Tunbridge Wells, The Longbow and it was to be their son Darren's first trip abroad with Chelsea. Richard asked Match to look after his son out in Sweden, fat chance of that I thought to myself. But I knew that he would be safe with all us lads from Tunbridge Wells and we wouldn't let Richard or Christine down, we never did! He got back safe and sound.

Left to right: Andy Warren and Darren.

Just waking up in Stockholm (Good-Morning) Andy and Match.

Tickets for the game in Stockholm were no problem, as Match's brother Andy had been living in the Swedish capital for about six years, so he had got us all the tickets beforehand. That was one problem solved before we even left England. We were now being joined on our tables in the corner of the airport bar by a lot of other Chelsea mates from other parts of the country. Dartford Trevor and his young son sat down with us, as did Brixton Charlie and Finney who were also making the trip together with a lot of other known faces. It was finally time for the plane to take off, we had all made our way through passport control and the checkpoints safely, even Andy had started to board the plane and was sobering up, things were looking good I thought to myself. At last, we were actually going to take off for Stockholm, or so I thought, though I should have known better!! The airport that morning was full of Chelsea supporters, it was like a home game at Stamford Bridge, it was going to be a huge airlift with about ten thousand people flying out to Sweden during the next 24 hours from different airports around the country. Figures vary on how many supporters made the trip but it must have been about 15,000 taking into account those travelling by land and sea. Stuttgart were taking just under 4,000. The players said after the match, that it was like a home match with Chelsea packing every corner of the small Rasunda Stadium that Wednesday evening in May. The total attendance was only about 30,000 and well over two thirds were Chelsea supporters. The plane trip went quite well, with a lot of people catching up with some lost sleep. The only real incident on the three hour flight was Besa nicking some little bottles of scotch and spirits from the Duty Free trolley when it was paraded down the aisle The pilot reported the incident to the local police in Sweden, and they were there waiting for us when the plane landed. I had heard that Ryan Air were not going to serve any Duty Free on the flight, but as they did it was a bit of a bonus to us lads who were not kipping. Anyway, the local police spoke to the pilot and stewardesses of the plane. I don't think they could be bothered with nicking any of us, they just asked us to pay for the drink that had been taken, and we all chipped in and did that. After a severe warning from the Swedish Old Bill that we could miss the match and be put on the next flight back to good old Blighty, all was once again fine. We all gave Besa a good old bollocking for being such a prat and nearly getting us all thrown out of Sweden before we had even begun and left it at that! Besa is one of our own kind and Chelsea through and through, and we all really love him to bits (in a Chelsea, brotherly sort of way that is!!) After disembarking finally from the plane, we all walked across the tarmac runway to where the little passport control office was, which was no more than a very large tin hut, Heathrow or Gatwick it certainly was not! Still, I suppose it served a sort of purpose in the Swedish sticks, as not many flights took off and landed during a 24 hour time span, perhaps five or six a day! But who cared, we were all somewhere in Sweden but still about 600 miles from where we wanted to be - Stockholm!! Nice one Sticky. Once we all got through the little passport control office without any more mishaps and through the tiny airport terminal, I turned to Sticky and said to him, "Mick (Sticky) I thought we were flying into Stockholm?" I should have known better knowing Sticky for about thirty odd years, will I ever learn!! "Not to worry Trev," said Sticky, "I have another idea."

"OH NO!!" I thought to myself.

"A rattler," came the cry from Micky "that will get us all up to Stockholm and to the game." Now actually Kristianstad Airport, where we all were, was about 15 to 20 miles from the small Swedish town of Kristianstad, so it was over to the great travel organiser in our group, Sticky, once again, to sort it all out. After a couple of hours of standing about outside the airport terminal freezing our bollocks off and a lot of confusion (why couldn't they have played the final in some nice hot country, I was asking myself?), about forty Chelsea supporters, some by now worse for wear, all got onto a local bus to take us all into Kristianstad. The Local bus service only went out to the airport to pick up passengers four times a day, another fact we all did not know!! So once you came out of the airport terminal, you were not allowed back into it, hence why we were all by now freezing. The temperature was below zero. I was glad to see that bus turn up, I can tell you!! We had been told there was a railway station in Kristianstad where we could all catch a train, with connections to take us on a long 12 hour journey into the Swedish capital, Stockholm.

The bus pulled up to stop at a set of traffic lights right in the town centre of Kristianstad, and as I looked out of the window of the bus, I saw Sticky (Micky Dunn), our travel organiser and all time entreprencur!! He was beckoning all of us off the bus with mad, frantic hand movements. We all jumped off the bus before the driver could pull away again from the traffic lights and legged it to the railway station. I learnt later why Sticky had got us off the bus - he had just ripped off the driver and nicked all his hard earned takings and fares. I had

133

wondered why the driver was swearing at all of us as we got off, and why he was radioing his headquarters for help! Oh well, such is life!! After roaming around the local bars in Kristianstad and keeping all our heads down from the local plod for a few hours, we all made our way to the station in dribs and drabs so that the Old Bill couldn't recognise anyone. It had already been sussed out that there was a train leaving for Stockholm at a certain time and that was good enough for us. We were being joined now by lots more Chelsea fans and as the train pulled into Kristianstad station, everyone and their dog jumped on to it. Of course no one had a ticket for the rail journey but that didn't seem to matter, the train pulled out of the station and we were all singing, 'Stockholm, Stockholm, here we come!'

The trains in Sweden all have bars on them and so there was a mass exodus for drinks - the locals on the train must have thought that the loonies had escaped from the asylum! It was mayhem with everyone helping themselves behind the bar, the stewards just couldn't keep up with the demand, and while they were serving one person with a couple of cans of lager, someone else was nicking three or four more cans and passing them about the carriages to their mates. The local Hectors (railway guards) just gave up the ghost, they tried to make us pay our fares but they gave up in the end. One Hector got really uppity and pulled Match into the guard's carriage with the help of a couple of other guards. However, we calmed the situation down by finding out that the guards had young sons at home who liked football. It cost us two T-shirts each for the four guards on the rattler and also some flags, but we all thought that was a good deal, as the Hectors were happy with that, and told us they would leave us alone for the entire journey to Stockholm, providing we didn't cause any trouble. Of course, we all agreed to that and after giving them a bottle of Scotch each (which was nicked anyway!) a truce was called. We all agreed we had got a right result as we were now travelling to Stockholm virtually for free. We pulled into Stockholm railway station at about seven o'clock in the evening and as the train came to a halt, all I could hear was a chorus of 'Chelsea, Chelsea, we are here', echoing over and over again. As we left the station and went into the Scandinavian evening air, all I could see was hundreds and hundreds of Chelsea fans milling about. It looked to me like a Saturday afternoon down the Fulham Road. There were hardly any Krauts to be seen, perhaps they were waiting for the darkness of the night to ambush us, I thought to myself, or perhaps they were not going to bother to turn up to support their team in a major European final? Were the Germans about to get revenge for the World Cup defeat of '66 or the war, and about to trick us? Then it happened, fuck me, we had only just got out of the station when about 300 Stuttgart fans came running at us from nowhere, armed with bottles and bricks and lumps of wood. Angus was straight into the action, cracking a couple of Germans over their heads with a half drunk bottle of Scotch that he was clutching. Down they went, and the English boots rained in on them. Suddenly, the local bars around the station, where Chelsea were drinking, were emptying and there were about two thousand English giving the Krauts a thoroughly good beating and kicking. The Germans couldn't have realised that there were so many Chelsea around, or surely they wouldn't have tried anything on. They got absolutely obliterated, blood and guts were everywhere and it was mostly Germans!! This big, fat German with a beer belly hanging over his shorts and 'Stuttgart' tattooed across his bare chest, smacked Andy Warren with a lump of wood that resembled a very large cricket bat, right over Andy's shoulders. I heard a 'crack' and Andy went crashing down onto the pavement. I thought at first that the Kraut had killed Andy, but then I saw Andy move and knew that he was just stunned. On seeing this, Angus threw me a bottle, and I ran up to the Kraut and smashed him straight across his German forehead. He went down like a lead balloon and blood spurted from his head wound, on seeing this the younger Chelsea fans put the boot into him. His yells of pain were heard in the still night breeze - some Germans tried their luck and got brave, but by this time it was hopeless for them, they were getting battered from every direction possible and were so heavily outnumbered it was a joke. The sound of police sirens began to fill the night air, but not before all the Krauts got a good hiding. I looked around the carnage and saw Match and a couple of London Chelsea, who I recognised as Finney's crew from Brixton, and Guy - Ian Cox's brother from Tunbridge Wells, they were running the last few Stuttgart supporters along the Stockholm pavements. I thought to myself 'Another victory for England over the Germans!'"

Cheer up Micky, we won! (Micky Dunn). And below Sticky Bunn also, with, Scandinavian girlfriend, whose name eludes me.

Now, before people start to look at a map of Sweden and start to give me a lesson in geography and tell me that the distance between Kristianstad and Stockholm is not 600 miles, but 300 miles, I would have to agree with them. YES, it's about 300 miles as the crow flies, but when you're on a Sticky-Bun (Micky Dunn) away-day it's not!! BELIEVE ME, it's not. From Kristianstad we continued our adventure and went onto Malmo, which is on the southern tip of Sweden, a distance of about 50 miles, then from Malmo through to the towns of Helsingborg and Halmstad to Goteborg about another 150 miles plus, and finally the rattler from Karlstad down into Stockholm, about another 200 miles. Like I say, about a 600 mile round trip, lovely scenery but around the sun to reach the moon. Oh well, at least we were in the Swedish capital at last, better late than never I told myself. Still, like I said before, lovely lakes, forests and scenery!!

After the ruck with the Stuttgart Krauts, I was hoping that the game the following evening would also turn out to be an English and Chelsea victory as well. But in my heart of hearts, I knew it would be a tough match and a close encounter for Chelsea, which it turned out to be. It had all quietened down a little bit now around the streets after the fracas with the Germans, and it was decided to try and find some digs to stay in and rest our heads for the night before the game (European Cup Winners Cup Final) the next evening. Besides, Mr Warren (Andy) now needed a good night's rest after the beating he had just received. We asked about for somewhere to stay but as per usual on these 'away' trips, everywhere seemed to be booked up. Then we had a saviour from a most unexpected source, Sticky's Scandinavian girlfriend, who was helping him sell his swag, said she knew of a hotel where there was a room. She gave us the address of the hotel and Match, Angus, Andy and myself made our weary way there. After getting lost on the Stockholm metro, we finally found the hotel in question, but by now there wasn't just the four of us, we had met up with a few more known Chelsea 'faces' from Tunbridge Wells who were also looking for a bed for the night. Namely, Bimbo (Ian Cox, the jockey), Spud Taylor, Kim Johnson and Guy. I thought to myself, "How on earth are we going to get into the hotel with this lot?" Then a plan was quickly hatched, it was decided that I went into the hotel by myself and booked a room for the night and the other lads would bunk in somehow. So we all had a whip round and everyone handed their Kronas over to me. I went into the hotel reception and Sticky's bird (true to her word) had come up trumps, the porter behind reception told me he had a room. The rest of the lads were holed up in a nearby bar waiting to hear from me. A touch of luck at last. I handed over the Kronas to pay for the room. I was directed to the room, which was on the ground floor. As I opened the door I noted the large double glazed window in the room opened up opposite to the bar where the rest of the lads were drinking. The lads could see me from the bar and I beckoned them over, one by one they climbed in through the window under the cover of darkness. I thought that there were only us Tunbridge Wells lads, but Bimbo had met some more Chelsea lads, who also had not got a bed for the night, and they came through the window as well. Eventually there must have been about 30 Chelsea fans in the hotel bedroom. It looked like a scene from a Marx Brothers film. Match, Angus and myself told everyone that if we all kept quiet, we would have a room for the night and would not have to sleep under the stars. A few bottles of spirits and cans of lager were downed and a bit of coke was snorted up some noses on that night, stories were swapped of past exploits and, of course, the story was told of our earlier confrontation with the Krauts. Bodies were everywhere in the small hotel room but eventually morning came - the morning of the longest and best day of my Chelsea life. It was also (I hoped) the last time I would ever have to sleep with Match and Andy, much as I love them (in the Chelsea family way!)

All the lads made their way out through the window and down the road to a local bar-cum-cafe, that was opening up, to get some grub for themselves. I made my way down to the hotel's breakfast bar and stuffed myself silly. Afterwards I went to meet the other lads in the bar for some serious drinking to get into the right frame of mind for the day to come. I bet when the hotel maids cleaned that room, they must have thought that there had been a pretty wild party the previous night but I didn't hang around to find out! We moved on from bar to bar and kept bumping into 'faces' we knew from back home and the Chelsea terraces. It always seems strange to me, but whenever you are abroad either with England or Chelsea, you always seem to run into the same old 'faces', although you don't always travel together. It was about midday and Angus, Match, Andy, Darren and myself were drinking in one particular bar, when who should walk in, but Eccles, Babs and their entourage. Eccles made a beeline straight for me and I thought to myself, "Oh no, what the fuck have I done to upset him?" My mind was full of flashbacks but all he said to me was, "Trev, you and the Tunbridge Wells lads meet up with me at 5.30pm, we're going to hit the Krauts." He told me where and when, and gave me a plan of where he expected us all to be in position at 5.30pm that evening and then he was gone. He was going from bar to bar, planning a massive attack on the Germans. When Eccles spoke, you listened, it was like being in the presence of a god amongst football hooligans. He looked immaculate that day, dressed in an Armani suit and Chelsea club tie. If you didn't know who Eccles was, you could easily pass him for one of the Chelsea players, even Babs had a suit on instead of his usual one sleeve T-shirt. Eccles later told me that he had been staying in the same hotel as the Chelsea team for the last two days, and over breakfast had been discussing tactics for the forthcoming Stuttgart game with the Chelsea captain, Dennis Wise and Gianfranco Zola. I thought to myself, I don't know about that, but later on he showed me a photo of himself with Dennis and Gianfranco, so I knew it had been the truth. Eccles is that sort of bloke, he can mix with the team and then mix with the likes of us. But Dennis and Gianfranco had definitely met Eccles, and I think Dennis spoke and still does to the Chelsea fans through people like Eccles. I remember, one occasion, when I went into an Italian restaurant just off the Fulham Road (it was a special occasion - I don't make a habit of going into Italian restaurants, too expensive). As we sat down a couple of bottles of vino were placed on our table. I said to the waiter, "I didn't order these" and he said, "Sir, the gentleman at the corner table sent them over for you and your lovely wife." I looked over to the corner table, and who should be sitting there, but Eccles, Roberto Di Matteo and Chelsea's most successful ever manager Gianluca Vialli. All three were smiling at me, I shall never forget that moment.

So, like I was saying, Eccles had a lot of inside knowledge within Chelsea Football Club as well as being a leader and legend on the terraces. 5.30pm arrived and we had made our way to where Eccles wanted us to be. It was on the corner of a small street with a main road running off it, about half a mile away from where the Cup Final was to be played later on in the evening. We were being joined by other groups of Chelsea who had all received similar plans and instructions from Babs and Eccles. I recognised some of the faces and knew that a massive battle was about to occur - I just hoped that Eccles had got his planning right! Mind you, he hadn't failed us before, I thought to myself. I was tapped on the shoulder. When I looked around there was a certain Mr Tracey Woods and the brothers Collins (Paul and Gary). They are really hard men from back home in Tunbridge Wells, so I thought that if a 'big off' was going to happen, then I would be safe with them around. In fact, I hadn't been so scared for years, the last time I had felt like that was when I was over in Ireland in the Falls Road. I knew a blood bath was about to happen, and it did!

After about 15 minutes, the sound of marching feet and shouting was drifting towards us all. And, as we looked up the road, coming straight for us, was, I estimated about 500 Germans. This was Stuttgart's main mob and they were being chased by about the same number of Chelsea fans and they were running straight into us. By this time, we were about 500 strong ourselves, and the Krauts were about to be sandwiched from the front and rear - a typical Eccles tactic, and one which had been used on many occasions at home and abroad. The Krauts didn't know which way to turn, they were surrounded and trapped like frightened rabbits in car headlights. Tracey walked slowly forward with Paul and Gary and we all followed. A lot more Chelsea jumped over a small wall, that they had been hiding behind, and a lot more came from another small side street. I had not seen this Chelsea mob earlier, but it was all part of Eccles surprise tactics and planning. Chelsea were everywhere and the Germans main crew were in the middle of us all. The Germans were by now about 20 yards away from us, they just stopped and made no move to run or charge us - they were supposed to be the elite of German soccer hooligans but to me it was obvious they were no use at fighting. We were now right next to them and not a word was spoken, it was very eerie. We all looked at each other, then I heard a crack of a punch followed by a few more, and I heard the words, "Take that you, Kraut bastard!" I recognised it as Eccles's voice. Then, all hell was let loose. I bottled a couple of German fans with the help of Match and Angus and they crashed to the pavement. Andy Warren, Paul and Gary stood over the Germans, putting the boot into them and were poised ready to take out the next German to move in their direction. The Germans were getting well and truly battered from every conceivable angle. They had nowhere to run or turn to, their fate was sealed. "A great result for Eccles and Babs," I thought to myself. However, it was a bit too calculated and planned for me, I always believed that football violence should be about the heat of the moment. The delay before tearing into the Germans was far too easy, and it was obvious that the Krauts did not understand what the rules of this particular game were. I'll give them their due, although they were heavily outnumbered that night, they stood and fought until they realised they were in 'shit street' and then panic set into them on a large scale. They bolted, each German decided to make his own bid for freedom from the dire situation they found themselves in. They should have stayed together and fought it out with us. They were now running everywhere, being pursued by Chelsea moving in for the kill. After a little while (which must have seemed like an eternity to the Stuttgart fans), the sound of sirens filled the evening air, and the police arrived on the scene. But, by the time they got to where the trouble had been, we were all gone and drinking in the bars close to the ground. The site of the trouble was like a battlefield, twenty, thirty, maybe more German bodies were lying on the road and pavements. The police were running over to them and trying to help them back on to their feet, and the ambulances were taking the more seriously injured fans to hospital.

Back in the bars and pubs, all us Chelsea were laughing and congratulating each other on a fine victory and on the great planning by Eccles and Babs. Yes, the Krauts certainly came unstuck that night in more ways than one. I made the score England 3 Germany O, 1-Nil the war, 2-Nil 1966 and 3-Nil Stockholm, 13 May 1998. Or was it 4-Nil? Did we once beat them in the Eurovision Song Contest? Oh well, perhaps not that one then!! We all made our way into the small Rasunda Stadium, just on the outskirts of Stockholm. Chelsea were in every corner of the ground - it looked like Stamford Bridge on a Saturday, but it was a Wednesday night in May, in Stockholm. Gianfranco Zola didn't make the Chelsea starting line-up on that evening, due to injury, but came on as a substitute after about seventy minutes. Seventeen seconds later, he won the European Cup Winners Cup with a glorious half volley from a Dennis Wise pass. The rest is written in Chelsea Folklore about this great, great Chelsea team. Chelsea were in complete control of the game after Zola scored. When the final whistle went, I was crying with years of pent-up emotions coming out of me. All those years of following Chelsea up and down motorways, getting relegated and cold winter nights in northern outposts, and now the final piece of the jigsaw puzzle (apart from winning the league that is) had fallen in to place. It was the icing on the cake - we had done it and won the biggest prize of all, what a moment!!! What a night!!! I hugged Match and he collapsed on the terrace, I thought I had crushed his ribs but he was OK. Total strangers were kissing and hugging each other - I'll never forget it. The 15,000 Chelsea fans danced out of the stadium to go on the piss in Stockholm, while the team drank champagne in the dressing room. Football doesn't get any better than this, three quotes from that night stick in my mind: Ernie (Dennis Wise) the Chelsea captain saying, "We'll have a nice team photo at the start of next season now." Gianfranco Zola saying, "I thought this is the moment Franco, take it. I hit the ball perfectly and it went where I wanted it to go, it was absolutely magnificent!" And the last quote of all, I think was from our goalkeeper that night, Ed De Goey (the Dutchman) when he said, "It wasn't a game I think in Stockholm, it looked like a game at Stamford Bridge. The fans were magnificent and so were we, both on and off the pitch!"

I didn't have to do a great deal of research to write this book, simply because I was there, and I know these people I have written about. Take for instance, Hickey, what a load of bollocks has been written about Steve! I know Hickey, I grew up with him in Tunbridge Wells and I have been involved with him from an early age to now. The Roebuck years etc. etc. A lot of people have written a load of rubbish about him, and they don't even know him, and have only perhaps heard of his name and are having a 'meal ticket' on it. Tossers the lot of them!! I was drinking with Hickey's sister-in-law the other day, and she was telling me how Hickey was getting on in Bangkok in his new found venture - a bar called 'The Dog's Bollocks'!!!

How on earth can people put into print something they certainly don't know anything about or understand.

In the 1994-5 season we all went to Lansdowne Road, Dublin for a 'friendly' game against the Republic of Ireland. The police intelligence units had tried to put a stop to hooliganism with the introduction of close circuit television and all-seater stadia, but not abroad. Hickey, buy this time was in paradise, he was now the leader of the Neo-Nazi group, Combat 18 and the idea was to wreck the match. I remember that before the kick-off, there was a feeling of hate and chants of, "No surrender to the IRA" and there were lots of Nazi salutes. Well the inevitable happened and Ireland scored a goal early on in the match - that was the opportunity for the rioting to start. Seats were torn up in the upper tier of the west stand and hurled at the Irish supporters below. The match was abandoned as hundreds of people tried to escape the carnage by running onto the pitch, the English police and Garda were trying to stop the rioting, but it was all too late. The tickets for the match had been readily available and segregation had become impossible. But this was Hickey in his element, Combat 18 and Neo-Nazi, yes, but violent, no. Well, not much!! And televised violence as well.

A couple of weeks later, we all went to Belgium, where Chelsea were playing Bruges in the European Cup Winners Cup. This time we couldn't get tickets for the match and about 2000 Chelsea fans went on the rampage. I remember getting detained until the game was over, and then being deported along with Garb, Angus, Andy Warren and Bobby Harbour. But not before we had wreaked havoc in Bruges and had the water cannons turned on us and the Belgian police batons had beaten us senseless! Still, I suppose it was what we all deserved!!

Hickey, Combat 18 and the Neo-Nazis were in great form that day, as well, as I recall. In the following round of the Cup Winners Cup in Spain, where Chelsea played next, tickets were sold to all-comers (big mistake). But when Chelsea conceded a third goal to Zaragoza, the inevitable happened. Fortunately the people of Zaragoza were saved by the Spanish police in their riot gear and the mayhem was quelled. But Hickey and Combat 18 had left their mark once again and how Hickey loved it!!!

A few books ring true, Mickey Francis's book 'Guvnors' is not a bad print about football hooliganism. I can remember the Manchester United clash and the other events that he has written about. And another good book is 'Hooligan' by Martin King and Martin Knight. This also seems to run with events, as I remember them. Another book I have read on the same subject is 'steaming In' by Colin Ward. I don't recall Colin at Chelsea, although he does say he only supported 'the Blues' for a couple of seasons and was a 'gooner'. I think Colin has done a lot of research, unlike other books. One book in particular comes to mind, written by a couple of brothers called Brimson, who claim to be ex-hooligans. Who are they? I've been involved closely in terrace life and soccer violence for over 30 years now, and I don't know them and neither do any of my mates. They say that they are Watford main crew leaders, excuse me, I've just fallen off my chair laughing. WATFORD? I don't ever recall Watford having a firm. Who was their main face? Elton John they'll be saying next!! Luton had a crew and Eric Morecambe was their leader. They certainly didn't have a crew the night we ran amok through Luton town centre, causing untold havoc and then burning out the rattler. They reckon people have sent in accounts of life on the terraces - bollocks - if they had been there, they would have known about it and seen it first-hand. Then they wouldn't have to rely on untrue stories, without any facts. Another book by the Brimsons is entitled 'Capital Punishment' and they reckon us Chelsea open up building society accounts to pay for 'away' travel and to pay for fines that had been imposed. More total bollocks! A whip round by Eccles or Babs on the 'away-days' special, yes but building societies, I think not!!!

And as for us Head-hunters hiring ourselves out to other football firms who needed some extra fighters with them, oh yeah? I can just hear my phone ringing now, "Trev, are you fit for Saturday, there's fifty quid in for you, by the way it's Harry the Dog from Millwall," I'd have been there like a shot, I DON'T THINK!!!! And as for another book by them entitled 'Derby Days', well it's beyond me, 'violence at Watford versus Barnet', a one man and his dog game. Did Elton John, the Watford chairman chase the Barnet chairman around the pitch side at the half-time interval whilst the marching band played on?? Nice one, I'll mark that fixture down for next season, that's for sure, yeah!!!

As far as I'm concerned, as to what I've seen in over thirty years of soccer violence, the top ten mobs and firms have been (and still are) in order, one to ten:

1. Chelsea (not being biased of course!)
2. West Ham
3. Millwall
4. Cardiff
5. Manchester United
6. Leeds
7. Arsenal
8. Manchester City
9. Bristol Rovers
10. Tottenham

In the early years, there were other teams who had tasty firms, for example Wolves, Stoke City, Everton and Portsmouth but the main firms are in the 'top ten'. Although most clubs had their leaders strongmen and nutters they were usually quickly disposed of on an 'away-day' to their patch.

The Sports Minister of the day Kate Hoey, has suggested that terracing be reintroduced to top British stadia, but has been slapped on the wrists by her boss, Culture Secretary of the day, Chris Smith about this suggestion. Now, we all know about the Hillsborough disaster on the 15th April 1989. It is etched in all football supporters' minds 96 Liverpool fans were crushed to death during an FA Cup semi-final. People will say you can't go back to the past, not after what happened that day, but I believe that you can! Yes, Hillsborough was a terrible disaster of mindless proportions, and many families are still having great difficulty coping with the loss of loved ones. Many said Hillsborough was safe, (which we now know was not the case) but is this what the fans thought? No, I think not. People will say Kate Hoey should sit down and shut up, but I'm not so sure. She's certainly got a point, the atmosphere at any game is better in standing areas. The swaying 'kop' at Anfield, the Chelsea 'shed', for example, standing and swaying shoulder to shoulder with a body of supporters' united behind their team. You can stand with the people you want to and don't have to be allocated places. Standing areas mean bigger crowds without having to invest millions of pounds. This could in theory, mean reduced prices. At least fans feel more involved in the games when standing up. That is why fans in seats at premiership games still stand in all-seater stadium. And fans who still want to sit down will benefit too, because they could still sit in their expensive seats, but no longer have to have excited supporters jumping up in front of them at the slightest hint of any goal mouth action. Let's face it, the Krauts have already done it. German stadia have complied with the all-seater demands of FIFA, whilst retaining standing areas for Bundesliga matches. Collapsible seating has been installed in Berlin, Dortmund, Leverkusen and Munich, which are like cinema seats and fold up around the crash barriers separating each step. And in Hamburg they have seats that can be tucked away into the steps at the same time, safeguarding them from damage and also doubling the capacity in the standing areas. That means extra money for SV Hamburg, as they can get about 4000 extra fans in at every Bundesliga match they play. So Mr Ken Bates, the extra money SV Hamburg spent on installing the special van-seats at their ground is soon recouped by revenue from their extra fans. They listened to their supporters, who don't earn much money and are used to standing, and prefer to stand at football matches anyway. And did not just develop their ground into a gigantic leisure complex. I'm sorry Ken, but it's a fact, some people don't like sitting down, the German clubs were happy to take on the extra cost for their supporters. Would that happen here? I don't know, but to me and other terrace folk, I have spoken to, it seems to be a good idea. Yes, you can use the Hillsborough argument against the German example, but the standing areas now are safe and are not a return to the terracing of earlier days. Technology has now been developed, which allows computer monitoring of pressure on crash barriers, entries and exits, so that any problems can be detected early. In addition, advances in computer software allow accurate projections of what will happen to crowds in emergency situations. It's obvious to me, that Premiership clubs would rather spend millions on new stadia than this cheaper option and not listen and get feedback from their own loyal (and paying) fans. If clubs don't want cheaper entry fees, then why don't they come out and say it!! Standing in a seated area is more dangerous than standing in a designated standing area. Look at the people who hurt themselves falling over seats, celebrating goals etc. They are not the people who persistently stand but those who get up in moments of extreme excitement, which is what (according to ground regulations) you're allowed to do. Let's admit it, some people prefer to watch their teams standing up rather than sitting down. The Germans have certainly opened up a lot of peoples' eyes and minds but not our own Government, as yet. Perhaps it's about time we all woke up and stopped living in the past. I personally prefer to stand at football matches but I'm not allowed to at the present time. Why should I pay my money and sit next to a complete (stranger), At the moment, it's a very unhappy marriage, yes, the Germans have found a way to stand and although I hate to admit it, they're one step ahead of us once again. I do not think that Kate Hoey has lost the plot completely. If you are neutral and weigh up all the facts, this idea is not a backward step and a turning back of the clock but a way to please everybody. Yes, Hoey had been impressed by the scheme in Germany, where a seated area can be transformed into terracing, which is said to be a much safer option than the old fashioned sloping concrete and is that wrong? I suppose some people will say that the fighting will start again before long and then fences would be brought back and that Kate Hoey, the Sports Minister of the day, is only vote catching. Well she's certainly got my vote and a few thousand other terrace folk, we are not persuasive activist or the lowest, common football fans, and, yes, I remember Heysel (39 dead), Hillsborough (95 dead) and Ibrox. Had these tragedies not happened, would anything have changed? I think not, we would still have terraces now. These tragedies must never be allowed to happen again, but surely in this technological age, they will not, but let's not be blindfolded and led by these sad events of the past, and, instead, listen to the Sports Minister and make up our own minds. Millions of pounds were wasted with Government grants and loans on an eyesore called The Dome, which could have been channelled into football and into something that the public wanted, not used on something that was doomed to failure from the very beginning of its short life. I've always enjoyed a good ruck on a Saturday afternoon, with my mates beside me, I suppose it's always been in my nature and in the world of middle class England that I grew up in. Chelsea have been my life for well over 35 years and I couldn't imagine life without Chelsea being some part of it. It would be like losing a member of my family, it's difficult to explain to any outsider this feeling inside me, but I know it's there and always will be. Chelsea is part of my life and in orders of importance come after my wife, my children Charlotte and Rhiannon, my mother. My blood is blue not red!!

Yes, I liked a punch up, but so did the people we fought on Saturdays, well mostly! So why condemn us and the violence? Didn't these people have a youth? Perhaps not! They should have been with me and us Chelsea on an excursion to some northern town for a crack and experience life and the meaning first-hand, then they might just have been richer for the experience. They might have understood a little of what us terrace lads were all about, it was our buzz after a boring week at work, a way to let it all go. We all did our bit during the week, but Friday nights to Monday mornings was our time and for thousands of young men even today, still is. Organised fighting will always occur, no matter where and when and what country you are in. Make no bones about that! It's just that at football matches, everybody takes more notice, because it's such a publicised event and fighting at football is illegal. Turn on the television in the evening and jump through the channels with your 'zub box', and I bet you'll find a couple of channels with violence on them. it's all part of our society, like it or lump it. Look at the news, read the newspapers, violence is part of our lives. I'm not condoning it, it's just the way it was when I was growing up and was a large part of my life. You have to make up your own mind about what's wrong or right, it's just that for me and thousands of others it was the right thing to do at the time and even now, it still is.

I recently went on a pilgrimage to the 'Mecca' of Stamford Bridge with the General and his tribe. Although we are both now season ticket holders, we both had to pay the inflationary prices for extra seats for our families. I took my daughters, Rhiannon and Charlotte, and the General took his son and daughter. We all settled into our seats in the new Shed stand and looked out towards the Matthew Harding stand. My daughter asked me where I used to sit and stand when I was younger. I explained to her where the Matthew Harding stand is now, there used to be a concrete terrace called the north stand and going into gate 13 to run and ruck with the away supporters was then the order of the day.

I do not know if my little darling understood me, but I hoped in my heart of hearts that she had taken in a little of what I was saying.

The next thing I knew, Garb's son had turned to the General and said to him, "So this is the famous Shed, is it Dad?" to which Garb explained that in a way it was still called the Shed, but the real Shed had been demolished and pulled down many years earlier and that only memories remain of it now. But it was where he and his blues-partner TD had done their apprenticeship and also where they had gained their infamous terrace lives. I think he understood what the General (his dad) was saying to him. New blood indeed!

All the youngsters were by this time getting caught up in the atmosphere. It's still exhilarating and magical, but it's not the same for Garb and me. It's very different to the early years, and, I don't think for the better, but our kids loved it! They were singing and chanting with the best of them, when Chelsea went forward during the match. Give me the old Shed and the old north stand any day - that to the General and me was what football was all about. I will never get used to the rows and rows of plastic seats, I suppose I'm from another era, but I think it was a better era. You may not agree with my opinion, but it's just the way I see things and always have done. After the match, the youngsters all wanted hamburgers and hot dogs, so we stopped just outside the ground to queue up for some food. Whilst I was standing at the hot dog stall, I felt a tap on my shoulder and a familiar voice said to me, "Trev, have the hot dogs and hamburgers for yours and the General's kids on me!" I looked around to see the General chatting away to Eccles. My daughters said to me, "Who is that man Dad? He's very kind."

To which I replied, "Sweetheart, that man's a god."

"What, someone like Jesus?" they said. I picked up both my daughters and kissed them on the forehead very hard and with a tear in my eye and a lump in my throat, I thought to myself, "How close to the truth they are! 'out of the mouths of babes'. We got our food and Garb, Eccles and I carried on our conversation with the younger Chelsea fans walking past us along the Fulham Road, in their replica shirts, blissfully unaware of who they were walking past, but happy in another Chelsea victory. The legends live on, and so too does terrace life.

## Epilogue

"Chelsea United, will never be defeated!" This was the cry that used to bring terror to the opposition's mob or crew, that used to face us on the battlefields of the terraces and the adjoining streets and roads to their grounds. This was our war cry as much as 'Over the top, lads' was the cry in the First World War. Most clubs, firms and mobs used to turn and run on hearing our war cry, and we then had to give chase. When they didn't run, and stood to fight and fronted with us, the fun and action really started.

I am not glorifying the trouble and violence in this book, but it was just the way it was for me and thousands like me, in my youth. I suppose people, on reading this, will say that the things we did were antisocial, but to me, it was all part of growing up, and I would certainly do it all over again, that's for sure!!!!

I remember arriving at some northern ground with Eccles and his entourage, and us Tunbridge Wells lads were waiting for the 'green light' from Eccles to batter the Northerners, and applauding Mr Greenaway to his seat. It was always good to hear Mick's cry of 'zigger, zagger' at some northern outpost. It always brought a warm feeling to one's body on a cold and bleak night, and made one feel at home. A great character was Micky, and sadly missed by all who knew him. I put Mick up there, alongside other Chelsea 'greats', Ossie, Zola, Bonetti, Chopper, Eccles, Babs, and Hickey in Chelsea folklore. I think Micky's smoking habit of about 100 cigarettes a day led to his final fate with that big, green turf in the sky. I believe that he suffered some kind of a stroke. But I will always remember Mick in his old 'Bud Flanagan' style coat that he used to wear, giving out his earth shattering cry of 'zigger zagger!' You could quite easily see Mick staggering into the Winchester Club in an episode of 'Minder', and being befriended by 'Arfur and Terry.

We now have 'one man went to mow', but on those hostile northern terraces in the mid sixties, when not so many Chelsea travelled to 'away' grounds, Micky's cry of 'zigger zagger' was a way of calling Chelsea fans together, and for me still is. I could have written lots more stores about my 35 years of following England and Chelsea, but, if this book is a succcss, I will probably write a sequel - To the Terraces Born 2 - Who Knows???

But, for now, I hope I have shared a little of the excitement and thrills, that for me were and still are my life, and always will be. Amen!!!!

*Football is not a matter*
*Of Life or Death.*
*It's much more important than that.*

BILL SHANKLY.